# Praise for Looking For My Good Face

"Rosemary and I have known each other over many lifetimes; in this one, we have been each other's teacher and student for nearly thirty years. Rosemary has helped me become a same-different-stronger-truer version of myself by providing a sacred and trustworthy space for me to face my fears and illuminate my path. Rosemary has acted as both cairn and compass on my journey to remembering who I am. She has been a faithful mirror, inspiring me to know and live my deepest truths. I am ever grateful for her Divine wisdom, her transformational toolbox, and unconditional love and support."

—Meaghan E. Mundy, Ph.D., Associate Dean of Students, Peabody College, Vanderbilt University

\*\*\*\*\*\*\*\*\*\*\*\*\*\*\*\*\*\*\*\*\*\*\*\*\*\*\*\*\*\*\*\*\*\*\*\*\*\*\*\*\*\*\*\*\*\*\*\*\*\*\*\*\*\*\*\*\*\*\*\*\*\*\*\*\*\*\*\*\*\*

"In Paul Simon's ***Bridge Over Troubled Water,*** he says, "When you're weary feeling small, when tears are in your eyes, I'll dry them all. I'm on your side, when times get tough, and friends just can't be found like a bridge over troubled Water I will lay me down." Rosemary Cathcart has been a bridge for many people. This magnificent book is her bridge to all of us. May it be on your side, be your friend and help you "sail on."

—Nancy M. Lorenzi, Ph.D. Retired Assistant Vice-Chancellor for Health Affairs and Professor of Biomedical Informatics, Vanderbilt University

\*\*\*\*\*\*\*\*\*\*\*\*\*\*\*\*\*\*\*\*\*\*\*\*\*\*\*\*\*\*\*\*\*\*\*\*\*\*\*\*\*\*\*\*\*\*\*\*\*\*\*\*\*\*\*\*\*\*\*\*\*\*\*\*\*\*\*\*\*\*

"I have been Blessed to share in Rosemary's ***Circle of Light*** for over 20 years, and I have literally, trusted her with my Life. Little did I know that our journey together would become the remaking of my true self, as she coaxed me into shedding the layers of accumulated protections and rationalizations. She walks her talk and she is the real deal! She helped me to know that the ***light*** I was searching for was already present inside of me. Amazing shifts will occur in your Life as you allow this calm and grounded metaphysical teacher to hold your hand as she guides you to becoming who you truly are! She knows what is true and what is possible. It always warms my heart when you are so open, loving and always for the other person!"

—Sande Churchill, MA, Ph.D., MCC, A True Human Seeker

\*\*\*\*\*\*\*\*\*\*\*\*\*\*\*\*\*\*\*\*\*\*\*\*\*\*\*\*\*\*\*\*\*\*\*\*\*\*\*\*\*\*\*\*\*\*\*\*\*\*\*\*\*\*\*\*\*\*\*\*\*\*\*\*\*\*\*\*\*\*

"Rosemary Cathcart may think she is just one person, but inside her dwells an intuitive counselor, a Spiritual guide, a wholistic healer, a talented author, a Pages of Shustah reader/interpreter, and a practitioner of many disciplines and modalities including Astrology, Numerology and Reiki. I don't know how she embodies all of this, but I and countless others are the Blessed beneficiaries. Plus, we get to do this big, grand Life together!"

—Eunice Colmore, Reiki Master, Healing Touch Practitioner, Canine and Equine Massage Therapist, and a Student of Everything!

# LOOKING FOR MY GOOD FACE

# LOOKING FOR MY GOOD FACE

## A Journey of Discovery

**What To Do When ~ Before You Even Ask Why**

**Rosemary Cathcart**

Story Mountain Media, an imprint of Crippled Beagle Publishing
www.crippledbeaglepublishing.com
Knoxville, Tennessee, USA

Cover design: Brittany Cline

Paperback ISBNs 978-1-965334-11-9, 978-1-965334-14-0
Hardcover ISBNs 978-1-965334-12-6, 978-1-965334-13-3
eBook ISBN 978-1-965334-15-7

Library of Congress Control Number: 2024922423

Disclaimer: To my beloved colleagues, if any material quoted here came from you and is not properly credited, please let me know since, in many instances, it came to me from a friend of a friend who did not share with me the origin of the work. If that is the case, I am sorry, and I thank you from the bottom of my heart, as your work has been shared in the spirit of cooperation and love for all mankind. No deliberate plagiarism was ever intended. In addition, certain words are capitalized because they are important, elevated, and distinctive in the fields of study and practices discussed in this book.

Printed in the United States of America

This is *your* indispensable guide to a healthier, happier, more joyful/productive/curious and passionate Life. These ancient and time-tested principles might make immediate sense to you, and you'll wonder why this book wasn't available sooner. (I wonder why, too!)

This book is dedicated to the curious ones, the students of life who believe in the endless Divine Mysteries; the seekers and the "out of the box" brilliant ones who carve out their own path, no matter how unusual that might be. If you're reading this now, then it's dedicated to you, my Fellow Travelers and Friends along the path, and to every client who has ever trusted me ~ this is for you!

# CONTENTS

# Introduction: Getting the Best Out of This Book

Hello, and thank you once again for picking up this book. It has been my long-time hope to create and to share it with you. My most sincere wish is that we all wake up to our best and most joy-filled, hope-filled faces every day. Since I want to make this book as user-friendly as possible, I think it might be a good idea to guide you through a typical first appointment with me right here in Nashville, Tennessee, "Music City, USA."

Your first appointment sets the tone for our entire relationship, and I want you to feel welcomed, comfortable, and at ease from the moment you walk in the door. As a long-time student of Dr. Milton Erickson, and routinely applying the techniques of Ericksonian Hypnosis, I know the work between the two of us begins the moment the appointment is scheduled. Unbeknownst to all but the most astute observers of energy, the transmission of energetic matter and intention begins at that moment of commitment. I will be thinking about you and creating your Astrological Chart ~ and of course, you will be thinking about and imagining what will come of our time together. This is just another extraordinary aspect of the level of Divine Magic that comes with our being Spiritual Beings in physical bodies.

Since I work through referral, I have a good sense that whoever sent you my way must think we will make a good match and that my skill set and temperament will work for you. I am always deeply grateful and rather astonished at the skills I've been allowed to develop over the course of my career, and my greatest joy is in being able to help people just like you! Above all else, I consider myself a healer who also just happens to be an Astrologer working with Numerology, Reiki, Emotional Freedom Technique (EFT), hypnotherapy, and an entire host of assorted esoteric modalities.

You'll find me in the suburb of Oak Hill where I live in a typical, late 1950s brick ranch. Imagine yourself now in your vehicle, pulling to the back of my driveway and finding the door, just as I explained when we spoke. I'll be greeting you at the door, while holding my dog Brady in my arms ~ else your entire appointment might be about chasing my frisky pup through the neighborhood! The office we'll be working in has the home's original, knotty pine paneling, making the environment cozy and quite welcoming.

After exchanging the usual pleasantries, I'll ask you to have a seat at my desk, and I'll hand you a copy of my "Consent for Treatment" form to fill out as I leave the room to get us glasses of water. Leaving the room is quite intentional, as I want you to fully settle in by yourself for a few moments. My hope is also that you'll become aware of the treasure trove of original artwork on the walls. Each grouping depicts one of the various areas of study I've been exposed to and most likely trained in to one degree or another. You'll find Buddhist, Hindu, Lakota Sioux, and Cherokee traditions well represented, along with candles, crystals, Angels, chimes, and a dedicated altar table covered in prayer requests and yes, still more crystals and chimes. The crystals in the dish on my desk are meant to be held while we're meeting, or not. If a certain crystal or stone calls to you, by all means, please pick it up and savor its effects while we are working together. The vibration of that particular piece is probably exactly what you need at that moment.

The crystals, the chimes, and the sacred artwork combine to keep the office area and me functioning at a higher than usual vibrational rate. I want that heightened vibration to keep me fully present so that I can assist you at the greatest possible level.

As I take my seat across from you, I'll glance at the consent form. Then I will explain that I start each session with a Blessing to set the tone for our time together. I will ask to hold your hands. As I take your hands, I will intentionally place my index fingers on your wrists' pulse points to help me gauge any level of internal stress ~ or lack of it.

After asking you to close your eyes and take several long, slow, comfortable, deep breaths in through your nose and out through your mouth, I will speak out loud the words to the Blessing I was given years ago from Spirit:

*I would like to ask for guidance for each of us, asking that you be led to seek whatever information, guidance, or healing that is most appropriate for your Life at this moment, asking that I be allowed to function as a Channel for that information and that guidance, asking that I see, hear, speak, and feel with love, clarity, and understanding in all situations. Thank you, and so it is!*

With emphasis and clarity, I will say these words slowly as I demonstrate what deep and concentrated breathing actually sounds and feels like. (If I can't be an example of what I am striving to share, I can hardly expect you, the client, to grasp the concept either.)

While I am holding your hands and saying the words to the Blessing, which is designed to open up the energetic pathways between us, other work will be happening. I'll use the moment to project a series of Traditional Reiki Symbols to your Third Eye and to your Heart Chakra to not only help you relax, but also to allow you to access the deepest knowing in your heart and mind about why you're here with me. It's not unusual for people to come for specific issues, only to get here and discover that something totally different rises to the surface to be addressed.

A big part of my job is to make you feel absolutely seen and heard, confident that my total attention is focused on you and only you. Being held in the gaze of someone genuinely interested in who and what we are is rare, but people fascinate me; I love their stories and the myriad ways they figure out any number of wacky situations. Please believe me when I say that I can relate to each and every one of your stories and situations. I commiserate with the beginnings, the middles, and the ways all of those trickier and sometimes uncomfortable situations end.

I approach each new client from the perspective that I might have only one shot with you, so I want to make our time together as valuable and worthwhile as possible. And yes, I always give homework and assignments, starting with the consent form, which gives me a chance to look at your handwriting, one more doorway into visiting the "real you."

Since I understand the significance of personal history and hereditary patterns, I always begin with a thorough in-take. If you're reading this on your own now, why not join in and actually begin our work together at this moment? Use an existing journal if you like, use the pages and space provided in this book, or start a brand new one dedicated to this next important chapter of your life. Please do not attempt to do this work electronically, as the written word using an actual pen and paper in your hand travels an entirely different route through the brain, and that's what we want to access now for the best possible mental and emotional outcomes.

Most likely, as I walk you through these steps, you'll begin to notice subtle internal responses to the questions and how you're feeling both mentally and emotionally as you write out the answers. Do your best to give this your full attention without extraneous sounds, a computer program, or any other electronic noise running in the background. It does make a considerable difference, and even if you're skeptical or tempted to argue with me, please just have the courage to trust the process.

Bear with me and write out the answers to the questions in the order they're asked.

The first question I ask is that you give me your full name at birth and your birthdate. This usually raises eyebrows since I've already taken this data and cast your Astrological Natal Chart prior to our meeting.

However, when a person is asked to give his or her full name and birthdate out loud, it's nearly impossible to be thinking of anything else but that. As humans, we are fairly undisciplined when it comes to our mind/brain circuitry and our ability, or lack of ability, to manage and to control our thoughts.

As you're speaking, I'll write down your name in the center of the page, with your birth date directly below in this manner:

Sally Marie Fletcher

7. 23. 1968

36/9

To arrive at this number, we separate each digit, then add them together.

$$7 + 2 + 3 + 1 + 9 + 6 + 8 = 36$$

We then separate that sum and add the digits to reduce the math to one numeral.

$$3 + 6 = 9$$

This number immediately tells me quite a bit about your Life path and what Numerological patterns you're working with for this go 'round. The number also lets you see a bit about how I work and the various things I bring into the mix. Nothing is random about your birth or your numbers or my process.

As we work together, I will tell you the value of each digit in your birth number pattern and the expected influence each might have. The numbers that make up your day, month, and year of birth create (through the formula explained before) what is called the Path of Destiny, sometimes also known as the Life Path Number, which offers a deeper understanding of the Spiritual Laws that govern this particular life journey/incarnation.

The next question is what is your mother's full name and the date of her birth? I can usually sense as you're responding what the general pattern of your connection to her is or was. I can usually tell at this point if she is still alive in physical form or if she has already made her transition into the realm of Spirit.

If the channel of communication between the two of us (you and me) has been established with ease and depending on the energetic strength and eagerness of your relatives in Spirit, I may or may not begin to hear and then to repeat to you dialogue from your deceased loved ones. I was trained to be a Full Trance Medium by the late Renee Wiley of Fort Lauderdale, Florida. However, I had to give it up for the most part because I could never hold a strong enough boundary between myself and those in Spirit who were so eager to push through with a message. Nine times out of ten, I would start choking and be unable to deliver a coherent message. Now, if someone is eager to come through, and they have manners enough to not make me choke, I am delighted to deliver a coherent message to an eager and receptive loved one. Even though it was exciting, Full Trance Mediumship was not a glamorous career choice!

Moving right along, I then ask the same questions about your father and your siblings, staying alert once again to your responses and the resonance in your voice. We unintentionally give a great deal away with our body language and the ways we speak. I feel quite fortunate to have been trained in a number of disciplines that help me pay attention to even the slightest nuance in behavior.

I hope you're following along and writing this down for your own benefit. If you are, you're now creating the basis for the type of in-depth work that is designed to take a deep dive into the purpose and the substance of your Life.

The more thorough my original in-take, the better prepared I will be to help you across the broad spectrum of your current Life, focusing also on your most heartfelt hopes, wishes, and dreams for the present and future.

I will now ask about your relationship status and go about the business of collecting that personal history as well. Everyone we are sexual with in this lifetime is a past Life partner, and we are connecting once again to continue the joy, to apologize, or to simply wrap up that connection. Everything in the Universe has a beginning, a middle, and an end. It is important to value each step along the way. With that in mind, I will do my best to gather, in chronological order, the names and birth dates of your former partners, marital partners, and your current partner. I'll also be collecting any actual wedding date(s) as a marriage or a commitment ceremony creates a third entity with a definitive Astrological pattern all its own.

I'll also take an inventory of any children you've given birth to or any you might have adopted. According to an esteemed former teacher of mine, a Kabbalistic Rabbi who was also an Esoteric Astrologer, our path into physical form follows an elaborate Cosmic plan. From this teacher I learned that when we are allowed to come back into physical form ~ because it is considered a gift worth honoring ~ we appear before the Nine Lords of Karma to review every Life we have ever lived. Since we view this from a Soul perspective and not from an individual personality perspective, we are much more open and alert to the Karmic overlays of each and every thought, decision, and action. Once our Life reviews are complete and the connections have been fully established, **we are the ones** who choose the parents, the time, date, and place of our births. We are allowed to see the first thirteen years of our lives, along with any possible illnesses or Life-altering situations, such as abuse or addictions we might be required to deal with. And despite any supposed issues or fears, we jump in courageously, ready to face destiny.

I realize this is a dramatically different perspective than our current Judeo-Christian beliefs, but I believe it's an accurate one. As I have done this work, sometimes for two and three generations in the same family, I can see the threads of truth in what my Kabbalistic Rabbi taught me so many years ago. I am Blessed to have been his student, and I honor his teachings.

Finalizing your in-take, I will be interested in your educational background and your current career path. Naturally, I'll be asking why you've made these educational and career choices and who might have influenced them.

Since most of us never take the time to say all of this out loud, let alone to write it down, my personal in-take for you also acts as an opportunity for you to revisit important decisions and various Life choices with a fresh perspective. The exercise offers me the perfect gateway to ask how I can best be of assistance to you. I will ask, "What is the most important thing you'd like to take away from our work today and going forward as we unlock all of the magic and the brilliance that is YOU?"

When you answer, our journey together begins in earnest, and I am all in, one hundred percent. My hope is that you are as well.

# Chapter One

## How to Get Out of Your Own Way

I was raised as a strict Irish Catholic and was the second youngest in a family of seven children. When I came home from school one day and announced to my mother, "Mommy, Mommy, God is making Baptists now! There's a new girl at school, and her name is Bonnie, and I want to be her friend, but if she's a Baptist, and we're all Catholics, am I allowed to be her friend?" My wise and patient mother knew immediately that my parents' strict Catholic teaching had gone a bit too far. She sat me down at that tender age and explained that there were many different religions Worldwide, but we all prayed to the same God. The news shocked me, but then I started looking at the World with more curious eyes. Sometimes, I was a bit too curious, like when I asked the clerk at the corner market if she was a Baptist, too. My mother was a patient woman.

If you're not Catholic, look up the prayer The Act of Contrition, and you'll have a better idea of the scope of indoctrination to which all budding young Catholics are subjected. Years later, in retrospect, the pressure is heartbreaking and still quite stunning, but it also makes me even more grateful that I was able to "escape" that deeply ingrained, childhood, religious indoctrination. No matter how well intentioned, I believe the severity and limited thinking was wrong and damaging, especially to my sensitive, impressionable Spirit.

Although he never set foot in any other house of worship other than a Catholic Church, my father had the wisdom to urge each of his children when they reached the age of thirteen to, "Go out and experiment in the World. Go to other churches and synagogues and see what you think!"

I did exactly that at the age of thirteen and made two new "best friends."

Patricia was a tall, slim, stunning girl with curly, short black hair and the creamiest chocolate brown skin I had ever seen. She was also a Southern Baptist, and she took me to church with her family many times. Sunday dinners with her loud, funny, and lovingly accepting family were not only a culinary surprise, but also a relaxing treat for my typically tense digestive system. I had never seen so many people at one dining room table in my life. Not only that, but they seemed to come and go with ease, since there didn't appear to be any set time for the late afternoon gathering to formally begin. Everyone who showed up came with a covered dish or a dessert, usually hot out of the oven. I remembered thinking one Sunday that I could surely get used to the delicious fun. It never ever occurred to me that I was the only white person at the table because they all made me feel welcomed. Patricia with the creamy chocolate brown skin and open heart was my "first Baptist." I adored her.

My friend Esther also had curly hair, but hers was the blonde-brown variety often found in Jews from Central Europe. Esther's parents, Fannie and Izzie, had made their money owning bakeries in New Jersey before retiring to Buffalo, New York. Tasty baked goods always waited for me on their kitchen counter. I was told I could have anything I wanted. No one had ever told me that at home about food. Their generosity and ease were a revelation. Their level of sincere acceptance and warmth toward me provided a safe haven for my tender heart. I was shocked one day at temple with Esther when I realized the incense they were burning was the same incense used at my Blessed Sacrament Church for the High Holy masses. I can still feel the thrill of that realization circle through my whole body. I couldn't wait to tell my mother.

As an Irish Catholic, I had been led to believe ~ even at that young age ~ that all Jews were "tightwads," which is "why they had all of the money." It's so damaging when statements like that are floated around carelessly in daily conversation. We often have no awareness of how we are hurting others for no good reason.

Esther's older brother had commented, a number of times, that if his parents hadn't "fed every sad sack who wandered by the store, they'd be rolling in money!"

Father Izzy's response was always the same, "Why bake bread if you can't share it with a hungry mouth? I love to bake. People love to eat!"

If I close my eyes right this moment, I can put myself right in the middle of their comfortable and inviting home and clearly see all of them. They were such good people. Esther was my "first Jew," and I absolutely adored her, too.

The point here is that you should not allow the religious orientation of your birth family to ever hold you back from exploring your true destiny. Respect your heritage. Honor it, but also use it as a platform from which to rise and to expand the edges of your Life. You are much more than one small and rigid designation of self. I am grateful to have begun this Life as a Roman Catholic, but I am beyond grateful to have been allowed to expand well beyond those suffocating, guilt-ridden, and shameful constructs. Being raised as a Catholic taught me to pray and to revere God, the Holy Spirit, and the Angels, and I am immensely appreciative. Besides, I really like being Irish and all that comes with that stubborn, determined, and talented nationality. I got out of my own way by learning from and respecting the religious ideas of others.

Now, let's talk about how you can get out of your own way.

## Gather Your Resources

The Universe is much larger than any of us can ever wrap our minds around, and yet we belong; we are a part of it all. The sheer magic of the Universe is an extraordinary soup of brilliant possibilities to which we have access ~ **if** we're led to explore. The first step is to be open to our curiosity. The second step is to remember that all great explorers start somewhere. The third step is to know **God's got us** and all is well.

*When we try to pick out anything by itself, we find it hitched to everything else in the Universe.* ~ John Muir

The oldest book of instructional knowledge on the planet comes from Jewish Mysticism and is called the Kabbalah. Kabbalah is an esoteric method and a discipline widely considered to be the most comprehensive reservoir known of "original Spiritual wisdom." The literal translation of the word *Kabbalah* is "that which is received." In other words, to receive we must be receptive, and in this teaching, that refers to revelation from God as received by Jews. As with all things religious, *Kabbalah* means many things to many people. It is a true ancient wisdom that reveals how the Universe and Life itself work and how they are meant to work in harmony with one another. As a course of study, the Kabbalah is a sophisticated teaching intended to be undertaken only after the student has become well versed in other areas of the Torah first as a basis for this deeper study.

The Torah itself contains both written laws and oral laws. The written portion of the Torah contains the first Five Books of Moses and forms the basis of the Jewish religion. As is the case with many esoteric teachings, the most intimate and important portions of the teaching must be done orally from teacher to student in person. I was told by my original Kabbalah teacher that "the written Torah is a sacred text bound together with a specific number of words. However, the Oral Torah would always be a living, growing organism of insight and wisdom that would deepen and expand in the presence of each unique teacher-student relationship and thus could never be captured on a page." There would be no Kabbalah without the Torah.

The Tree of Life is the primary mystical symbol of Kabbalistic teaching. The Tree itself is the structure of ten Sephiroth, arranged in a set of three pillars. As with many ancient teachings, names can be spelled in many ways, and all are commonly accepted. Contained within the Sephiroth, commonly referred to as the branches of the Kabbalistic Tree of Life, are the keys to the study of many esoteric disciplines. I have always been immensely fascinated by how the Sephiroth of the Tree of Life corresponds so closely to the Psalms of the Old Testament. To me this is just another link proving the connection of all Life, including our various traditions and religions, whether they be Jewish or Christian.

In my original study of the Kabbalah, I learned from my teachers that the book and the study dated back to 2 A.D. However, a quick Google search of the name now reveals that "The Kabbalah developed between the sixth and thirteenth centuries among the Jews in Babylonia, Italy, Provence, and Spain." Choose whatever dates work for you. I'll simply explain what I know about it based on the teachers and Kabbalistic Rabbis with whom I was privileged to study. I realize that with many esoteric disciplines, the actual written record of these practices sometimes took several hundreds of years to catch up to the actual events and practices. According to my teachers, the Kabbalah as a spiritual study was taught to a practicing Rabbi once he had attained the age of forty, was married, and was in an ongoing sexual relationship. Such was considered to be the magnitude of power. If one was not sexually active and had not had previous study upon which to base the new insights, he could not manage the surge of explosive and powerful energy that accompanies this teaching. Traditionally, the teaching of the Kabbalah was shared only with an eldest son by a father who was also a practicing Rabbi. It was considered to be a rite of passage and a privilege to be taught these important and mystical skills. The oldest religions have remained strong and consistent throughout history for many reasons. Not every piece of information is meant to be shared with the masses.

As a perpetual student and someone privileged to look at life from any number of vantage points, I consider the "Esoteric Sciences" to include Astrology, Numerology, and the study of Symbology, among others, to be Sacred teachings. I was heartened to discover all of these duly represented in the original Kabbalistic teachings.

There should be a noticeable and much hoped for internal shift when we put aside all of our fears and open to a much broader Divine scope of things. And, yes, I will always capitalize *Divine*. Our inner guidance system will keep us on track. Please trust that. Being curious about the Kabbalah, realizing that Astrology is not sinful, and understanding that reading cards does not mean that you've sold your soul to the devil can be quite liberating and a healthy step forward in your personal evolution toward wholeness.

# Action Steps

Physically write a list of everything your family of origin warned you about "out there in the big, scary world," and use that as an excellent starting point. Also make a note of what their warnings were supposed to lead to, and don't skimp on any of those horrible details or threats about "never getting into Heaven with behavior like that!" Use the journal pages provided at the end of this chapter, or begin writing in your own journal if you prefer ~ but start writing this out with pen in hand, please! Hopefully, I will address those issues or at least touch on them enough to provide a decent opening for you to move through on your journey toward wholeness. This is a great way to start your personal journal of discovery. Consider reading and working through this book to be a courageous adventure with Divine safeguards. I would never intentionally present anything harmful to anyone, ever. But I do hope to make you curious and brave.

1. The first step is to be open to our curiosity. How can you be open to your curiosity?

2. The second step is to remember that all great explorers start somewhere. What small steps can you take in the next few moments or days to start exploring your full potential? Where and how can you start exploring?

3. The third step is to know God's got us and all is well. Write a list of evidence from your Life (past or present) that reminds you that God loves you and will protect you.

# Chapter Two

## Astrology

My first introduction to the wisdom seekers who embraced the importance of the stars were those three Wise Men who followed the signs and the stars to lead them to that tiny babe in a manger. I've always thought of the Three Wise Men as Astrologers. Then there was my mother, Virginia, who studied Astrology when I was a mere child of seven years. These four brilliant guardians of my galaxy paved the way for me to study something that I still find to be a brilliant portal into every aspect of Life. Astrology is a Lifetime study, and I learn each time I prepare a new chart for a client.

There are basically ten Planets, including the two "Lights" (the Sun and the Moon), which we all share in our individual birth charts. The Astrological Wheel is composed of twelve divisions called "Houses," which govern different aspects of our lives. In addition to the Planets, we have the North and South Nodes of the Moon and a number of Asteroids that have varying implications as to the overall patterns of our charts and our lives. Inherent in the study of Astrology is the study of numbers. Pay attention to the repetition of patterns as you begin to study your own chart.

I've created a perfect beginner's study guide to Astrology, which may whet your appetite to go further into this ancient divination tool. Use your birthday (find in the middle column) to identify your sign and symbol (left column) and planet and ruler (right column). The next page shows a pictorial reference chart.

If you want to accurately calculate your chart, there are many online services available to create your Natal Birth Chart for little or no cost. Using that as the basis for your study, you will be able to map out, in detail, the nuances of what you look like from an Astrological perspective. My favorite chart system is Placidus Tropical, so please use that system for your Astrological chart.

Review the following diagrams and materials, and then take the Actions Steps at the end of this chapter. Take your time and refer back as often as possible to your reference materials. Then deepen your sense of self and begin studying your own Astrological profile. The more we know about how we tick and what we need to create the best life possible, the better.

## The 12 Signs

| Sign & Symbol | Usual Dates | Planetary Ruler |
| --- | --- | --- |
| Aries, Ram | March 20 to April 19 | Mars |
| Taurus, Bull | April 19 to May 20 | Venus |
| Gemini, Twins | May 20 to June 21 | Mercury |
| Cancer, Crab | June 21 to July 22 | Moon |
| Leo, Lion | July 22 to August 23 | Sun |
| Virgo, Virgin | August 23 to Sept 22 | Mercury |
| Libra, Scales | Sept 22 to Oct 23 | Venus |
| Scorpio, Eagle | Oct 23 to Nov 22 | Pluto/Mars |
| Sagittarius, Archer | Nov 22 to Dec 21 | Jupiter |
| Capricorn, Goat | Dec 21 to Jan 20 | Saturn |
| Aquarius, Water Bearer | Jan 20 to Feb 19 | Uranus/Saturn |
| Pisces, Fishes | Feb 19 to March 20 | Neptune/Jupiter |

# THE 12 SIGNS

| | | |
|---|---|---|
| **Aries** March 20 to April 19 | **Taurus** April 19 to May 20 | **Gemini** May 20 to June 21 |
| **Cancer** June 21 to July 22 | **Leo** July 22 to August 23 | **Virgo** August 23 to Sept 22 |
| **Libra** Sept 22 to Oct 23 | **Scorpio** Oct 23 to Nov 22 | **Sagittarius** Nov 22 to Dec 21 |
| **Capricornus** Dec 21 to Jan 20 | **Aquarius** Jan 20 to Feb 19 | **Pisces** Feb 19 to March 20 |

# The Astrological Wheel

My go-to chart is *Natural Chart Wheel with House & Sign Keywords,* Symbols/Signs North Hollywood, California 91607. This recreation offers a clearer image with easier readability.

# The Elements & Qualities

The twelve signs are divided into four Elements: Fire, Earth, Air and Water. The twelve signs are also divided into three Qualities: Cardinal, Fixed and Mutable. The Elements and Qualities add a deeper substance to the descriptions of the temperament of each person.

The triplicities, so called because there are three Fire signs, three Earth signs, three Air signs and three Water signs. These signs are all harmonious with each other within each grouping, and they are all 120 degrees apart from the signs within each group.

Elements (triplicities) are signs which are 120 degrees apart and create a sense of harmony.

Fire: The Spiritual Realm ~ Aries, Leo and Sagittarius Earth: The Physical Realm ~ Taurus, Virgo and Capricorn Air: The Mental Realm ~ Gemini, Libra and Aquarius Water: The Emotional Realm ~ Cancer, Scorpio and Pisces

The Elements & Qualities

|  | FIRE | EARTH | AIR | WATER |
|---|---|---|---|---|
| CARDINAL | ♈ ARIES | ♑ CAPRICORN | ♎ LIBRA | ♋ CANCER |
| FIXED | LEO ♌ | TAURUS ♉ | AQUARIUS ♒ | SCORPIO ♏ |
| MUTABLE | ♐ SAGITTARIUS | ♍ VIRGO | ♊ GEMINI | ♓ PISCES |

## KEY WORDS AND CATCH PHRASES

| *Sign* | | *Planet* | |
|---|---|---|---|
| *Aries:* | I AM. Do it now. | *Mars:* | Never say fail. |
| *Taurus:* | I HAVE. Paid in full. | *Venus:* | Forgive and forget. |
| *Gemini:* | I THINK. Let's go places. | *Mercury:* | Talk it over. |
| *Cancer:* | I FEEL. Dinner is served. | *Moon:* | Mother knows best. |
| *Leo:* | I WILL. Take my heart. | *Sun:* | Watch my smoke. |
| *Virgo:* | I ANALYZE. Save the pieces. | *Mercury:* | Think it over. |
| *Libra:* | I BALANCE: You are welcome. | *Venus:* | Thank you, my dear. |
| *Scorpio:* | I DESIRE. Enclosed find check. | *Pluto:* | Do it my way. |
| *Sagittarius:* | I SEE. Laugh, clown, laugh. | *Jupiter:* | Plenty for everyone. |
| *Capricorn:* | I USE. Try, try again. | *Saturn:* | On your knees. |
| *Aquarius:* | I KNOW. Room for all. | *Uranus:* | Let us advance. |
| *Pisces:* | I BELIEVE. Wait for me. | *Neptune:* | I wonder why? |

## MINI-SKETCHES OF THE PLANETS

*Sun*: The Ego; eternal self; giver of Life; husband (in a woman's chart).

*Moon*: The Emotional Mind; instincts; change; women; wife (in a man's chart).

*Mercury*: The Communicator; reason, awareness.

*Venus*: Beauty; love, grace; cohesion; sense of values.

*Mars*: Energy: drive; aggression; the warrior.

*Jupiter*: The Sportsman; the gambler; the lawyer; the minister.

*Saturn*: The Teacher; the judge; restriction through responsibility.

*Uranus*: The Awakener; the rebel; the reformer; independence.

*Neptune*: The Dissolver; imagination; illusion; glamour; the dreamer.

*Pluto*: The Redeemer; the revolutionary; the anarchist; the extremist.

## THE DECANATES

Each sign contains 30 degrees. They are divided into 3 *decanates* of 10 degrees each. The decanates stay within the triplicity of the sign. For example:

*Aries*

1st decanate: Aries—ruler, Mars

2nd decanate: Leo—ruler, Sun

3rd decanate: Sagittarius—ruler, Jupiter

If you had a planet in 14 Aries, it would be in the Leo decanate, having Aries characteristics with Leo overtones, and having the Sun as a subruler. If you had a House cusp at 21 Aries, it would be in the Sagittarius decanate; your attitude toward the affairs of that House would be Arien with Sagittarian overtones, and having Jupiter as subruler.

Using the decanates gives a finer shading to your interpretation.

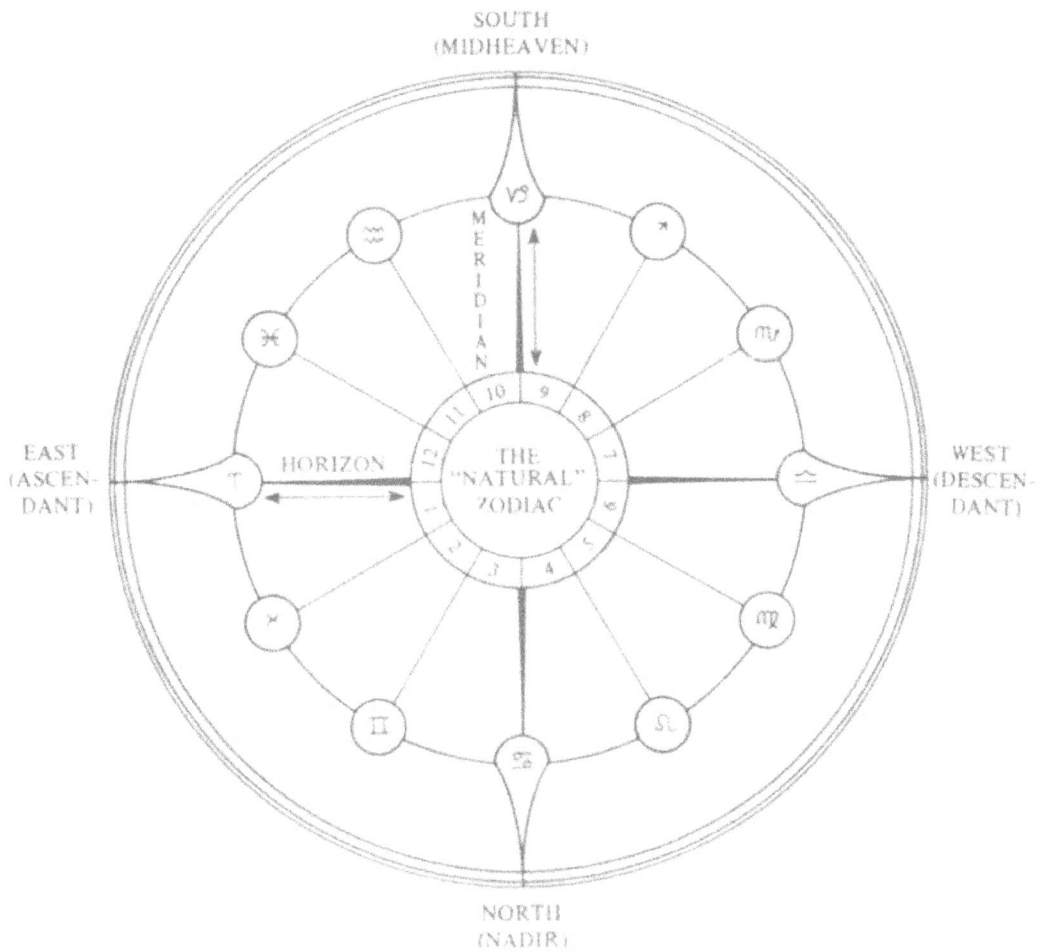

Source: Patricia G. Crossley, *Let's Learn Astrology*, published 1972 by Exposition Press, Inc. 325 Kings Highway, Smithtown, New York, 11787.

# Elements and Qualities

The twelve signs have been divided into four Elements–fire, earth, air and water–and three Qualities: cardinal, fixed, and mutable. The Elements and Qualities add to the description of the temperament of the native.

The *triplicities*–so called because there are three fire signs, three earth signs, three air signs and three water signs–are harmonious with each other within each grouping. Each sign is 120° from the other signs within its group.

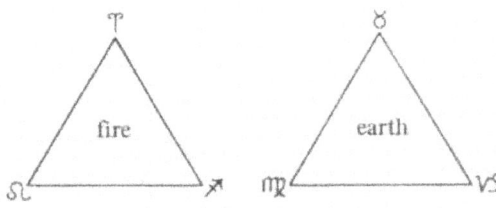

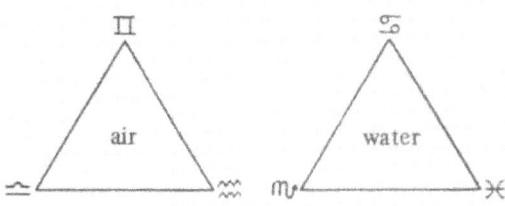

Elements (triplicities). Signs are 120° apart. Δ (Harmonious).

Fire: spiritual realm    ♈ ♌ ♐
Earth: physical realm    ♉ ♍ ♑
Air: mental realm    ♊ ♎ ♒
Water: emotional realm    ♋ ♏ ♓

The *quadruplicities* are so called because there are four in each group.

Qualities (quadruplicities). Signs are 90° apart. (Inharmonious, activating or irritating).

Cardinal: activity    ♈ ♋ ♎ ♑
Fixed: stability    ♉ ♌ ♏ ♒
Mutable: changeability ♊ ♍ ♐ ♓

The four *angles* are very important and very sensitive places in a chart. The angles are:

The Ascendant:       These
   First House cusp (East)    are the
The Midheaven (M.C.):    most
   Tenth House cusp (South)    sensitive
The Descendant:
   Seventh House cusp (West)
The Nadir (I.C.):
   Fourth House cusp (North)

Both groups fall into a natural order, as follows:

| Signs | Qualities | Elements | |
|---|---|---|---|
| ♈ | Cardinal | Fire | CF |
| ♉ | Fixed | Earth | FE |
| ♊ | Mutable | Air | MA |
| ♋ | Cardinal | Water | CW |
| ♌ | Fixed | Fire | FF |
| ♍ | Mutable | Earth | ME |
| ♎ | Cardinal | Air | CA |
| ♏ | Fixed | Water | FW |
| ♐ | Mutable | Fire | MF |
| ♑ | Cardinal | Earth | CE |
| ♒ | Fixed | Air | FA |
| ♓ | Mutable | Water | MW |

44

# Astrological Planets and Their Meanings

**The SUN:** The most powerful body in the solar system. It represents the *real self*, and all males in one's Life. It is the masculine principle, vitality and ego. Ruler of ***LEO Sun Signs***

**The MOON:** Next to the Sun in importance, it is linked with our conditions and emotional fluctuations and represents all females in one's life. It is the feminine principle, our instincts, and receptivity. Ruler of ***CANCER Sun Signs***

**MERCURY:** *The Winged Messenger.* It represents objective awareness, communication, intellect and adaptability. Ruler of ***GEMINI and VIRGO Sun Signs***

**VENUS:** *The Planet of Love.* It represents females, loved ones, artists, harmony, ease and attraction. Ruler of ***LIBRA*** and ***TAURUS Sun Signs***

**MARS:** *Planet of War.* It represents males, soldiers, mechanics and surgeons. Joint ruler of ***ARIES*** and ***SCORPIO Sun Signs.*** It governs action, aggression and courage.

**JUPITER:** *The Great Expander.* It enhances whatever it touches, for good or bad. Joint ruler of ***SAGITTARIUS*** and ***PISCES Sun Signs***, it is optimistic, visionary and devoted.

**SATURN:** *The Lord of Karma.* It represents older males and statesmen; governs discipline, restriction, tradition and systems of all kinds. Joint ruler of ***CAPRICORN*** and ***AQUARIUS Sun Signs***

**URANUS:** *The Great Awakener.* It rules inventors, reformers, disruption, originality and the unexpected! Ruler of ***AQUARIUS Sun Sign***

**NEPTUNE:** *The Great Dissolver.* It rules mystics, prophets, visionaries, idealism, imagination, confusion, delusion and inspiration. ***Ruler of PISCES Sun Sign***

**PLUTO:** *The Great Transformer.* It rules groups, organizations, Spiritual leaders, regeneration, transformation and domination. Discovered in 1930, it's a newbie! Ruler of ***SCORPIO Sun Sign***

**CHIRON:** *The Wounded Healer.* Rules philosophy and healing and represents the principle of holistic understanding. Named after a centaur, it was discovered in 1977.

# Astrological House Overview

Here's a brief description of each of the 12 houses of the chart:

**1st.** House which is determined by your Ascendant/Rising Sign based on your time of birth and sets the entire chart in motion, it is the hour of 6 AM and is the East. It represents your personal self, appearance, how you are perceived by others, temperament, instinctual desires, and overall health. The natural ruler is Aries.

**2nd.** House represents possessions, resources, finances, financial security, self-esteem, what becomes more valuable to you over time and your over-all values. The natural ruler is Taurus.

**3rd.** House relates to mental expression, learning, critical and logical thinking, your ability to communicate and share ideas via writing and speaking, short trips and siblings. The natural ruler is Gemini.

**4th.** House is all about your home, family, mother, nurturing, emotional security, safety, identity and the heritage you leave. It represents the Nadir or North and is the hour of midnight on the chart wheel. The natural ruler is Cancer.

**5th.** House represents how you sparkle in the World, children, romance, love affairs, speculation and entertainment. The natural ruler is Leo.

**6th.** House is the house of "service" and governs occupation, employees, work environments, self-improvement, tendency toward illnesses and small animals. The natural ruler is Virgo.

**7th.** House governs "others/the public" as in marriage partners, business allies as well as open enemies and rivals. It is your professional "network", clients, and co-workers. It represents the Descendant or West and is the hour of 6 PM on the chart wheel. The natural ruler is Libra.

**8th.** House is the house of our deepest emotional wounds, sexual desires, power, endings, physical death, taxes, insurance, finances and possessions inherited from others. This is the house of transformation. The natural ruler is Scorpio.

**9th.** House is the house of laughter, Mother Nature, the abstract mind, dreams/visions, long journeys, philosophy, religion/faith, law/truth and visions of the future. The natural ruler is Sagittarius.

**10th.** House is all about reputation and personal honor, the profession/career, employers and parents. It is the house of social status, authority, maturity and wisdom and generally represents the father. It is the Midheaven of the chart and is the hour of 12 Noon, located in the South.

**11th.** House is the house of our deepest aspirations, uniqueness. Friends/kindred spirits, hopes, wishes and social groups. The natural ruler is Aquarius.

**12th.** House represents places of confinement such as hospitals and institutions, hidden enemies, secrets and secret organizations. This is the house where hidden fears, hidden karma and isolations hold us captive until we are liberated by our Spirituality and the gift of Grace from the Divine. The natural ruler is Pisces, the final sign of the Zodiac and the "container" of all that has gone before.

# Action Steps

Once again, physically write down your date of birth again, looking at it now with a fresh set of eyes. Use the journal pages provided here, or you may write this down in your own journal.

1. What is your Sun Sign?

2. What is the Symbol for your Sun Sign?

3. What is the Ruling Planet of your Sun Sign?

4. What is the Ruling Planet of your Ascendant/Chart?

5. Consult the Chart Wheel, the Elements & Qualities and the Planetary Keywords for my in-depth knowledge.

6. Give yourself some time to let this information sink in and notice any of your feelings and any emotions that might arise.

# Chapter Three

## Numerology

The magic of numbers is as important to the overall pattern of our lives as is Astrology, and the influence of numbers is something I always consider during my client intake process. Over time, I've had the opportunity to see firsthand how the numbers of your Life ~ plus your birthdate, the numerical value of your original name at birth and major milestones in your Life ~ all play out in the unfolding journey of Life.

> *Each day is a new beginning*
> *another chance*
> *to learn more about ourselves,*
> *to laugh more than we did,*
> *to accomplish more*
> *than we thought we could,*
> *to be more than we were before.*
> ~ Unknown

We live in numerological cycles of 1 through 9 + 0, which makes up the entire spectrum of numbers, no matter where you live or what language you speak. The study of numerology began when Life began, because as we know from Genesis, the first book of the Hebrew Bible and the Christian Old Testament, "In the beginning was 1." The vibrations then began, and the number 2 appeared ~ creating the first pair ~ and ushered in the real beginning of Universal Geometry. According to *The Secrets of Numbers* by Vera Scott Johnson and Thomas Wommack, "Reference to numbers as metaphysical abstractions can be found in every ancient civilization known to man, including Egyptian hieroglyphics dating back to 3100 B.C. Numbers were used by the Chaldeans, Phoenicians, Chinese, Hindus, Hebrews, and early Christians. The rituals and writings of all the world's major and minor Spiritual and religious movements have used the abstract symbology of numbers. The Bible is a prime example, with its reference to numerological symbology, including the ***Trinity*** and the entire book of ***Revelation,*** which is a feast for numerical and Numerological symbolists."

Numbers by themselves represent *Universal Principles* through which all things evolve and continue to grow in cyclic fashion. The study of *Esoteric Numerology* is the art and the science of understanding the spiritual significance and the orderly progression of all manifestation. Every word or name vibrates to a number, and every number has its own inner meaning. The letter and number code, when rightly understood and then applied, brings us into a direct and closer relationship with the underlying intelligence of the Universe.

We are meant to live in a specific, sequential order. The idea being, of course, that we learn, mature, and gather skills and wisdom all along the way. At least that's the "theory" of sequential growth. We can only hope it's true and individually do our parts to grow into open-minded, compassionate people while working out our own Karmic life lessons.

Pythagoras of Samos (570-495 BC) was an ancient Ionian Greek philosopher and the eponymous founder of Pythagoreanism. According to those who followed his work, his political, scientific, and religious teachings were well known in Magna Graecia and influenced the works of Plato, Aristotle, and ultimately through them, Western philosophy. His many important developments included the areas of mathematics, astronomy, and the theory of music. It is interesting to put into the historical timeline that what we refer to today as Pythagoras's Theorem was known to the Babylonians one thousand years prior, but Pythagoras may have been the first to actually prove it. The theorem itself states that the square of the hypotenuse of a right-angled triangle is equal in area to the sum of the squares of the other two sides.

I've always had an uncanny sense that everything in the Universe owes its existence to the presence of numerical vibrations and that everything ultimately reduces to the value of a number. Take a look at the materials below and see if you can apply them to your own Life.

Write out your birthday like this: September 17, 1995. Then use only numerals like this: 9 – 17 – 1995

Now break apart those numerals like this: 9 1 7 1 9 9 5

The goal will be for you to determine your Destiny Number, which is derived by adding all of the single digits from your birth date together and then reducing them to the lowest numerical value. For instance, our example here is a public figure, Patrick Mahomes, currently the quarterback for the Kansas City Chiefs. His birthdate looks like this:

$$September\ 17,\ 1995$$
$$9 + 1 + 7 + 1 + 9 + 9 + 5 = 41$$
$$4 + 1 = 5,\ so\ his\ birthdate\ reduces\ to\ a\ \#\ 5.$$

Numerologists express these sums differently by group numbers, but the results are the same.

9 + 8 (digits of the day of the month) + 24 (digits of the year) = 23, which, if the two numbers 2 and 3 are added together, again equals 5.

To further illustrate, here are more examples of calculations of Destiny Numbers:

December 16, 1975, looks like this ~ December (3) + 16 + 1975 = 3 + 1 + 6 + 1 + 9 + 7+ 5

$$3 + 7 + 22 = \#\ 32$$
$$3 + 2 = \#5$$

June 19, 2001, looks like this ~ June (6) + 19 + 2001 = 6 + 1 + 9 + 2 + 0 + 0 +1

$$6 + 10 + 3 = 19$$
$$1 + 9 = 10$$
$$1 + 0 = \#1$$

Looking at the Destiny chart below, knowing that Mahomes is a #5, we see that he is an Adventurer whose Key Impressions are Freedom and Movement. His ruling planet is Mars.

| Destiny | Personality | Key Impressions | Ruling Planet |
|---------|-------------|-----------------|---------------|
| # 1 | Pioneer | Leadership/Independence | Sun |
| # 2 | Helpmate | Understanding/Adjustment | Moon |
| # 3 | Artist | Expression/Communication | Mercury |

| # 4 | Builder | Discipline/Organization | Earth |
| # 5 | Adventurer | Freedom/Movement | Mars |
| # 6 | Harmonizer | Responsibility/Healing | Venus |
| # 7 | Mystic | Analysis/Solitude | Saturn |
| # 8 | Executive | Abundance/Power | Jupiter |
| # 9 | Metaphysician | Compassion/Universality | Vulcan* |

"Master Vibrations" 11, 13, and 22 are indicators of outstanding abilities for leadership and accomplishment, indicating that more is expected of these individuals than the average person. It also indicates that extra energy is always available, but if the "going gets too tough," simply reduce the number to its lowest vibration.

| # 11 | (2) | Visionary | Revelation/Idealism | Neptune |
| # 13 | (4) | Chosen | Spiritual Mastery/Able | Pluto |
| # 22 | (4) | Genius | Material Mastery/Realism | Uranus |

My original Numerology teacher, M. Carroll Owen, insisted on the discovery of the planet Vulcan (#9), and she was not a woman to be trifled with, in physical form or "beyond the veil." In deference to her extraordinary wisdom, I always include Vulcan in my list of Ruling Planets as a way to honor her. Much of the Numerology materials presented here come from my studies with her and her "Digital Synoptic" method of computing numbers. Digitology refers to updating the ancient science of Numerology as an exact yet simple way to translate your birthday and name into simple number values.

**Table of Month – Vibration Values**

January = 1

February = 2

March = 3

April = 4

May = 5

June = 6

July = 7

August = 8

September = 9

October = 1 (1+ 0 = 1)

November = 2 (1 + 1 = 2)

December = 3 (1 + 2 = 3)

The Synoptic defines vibrational values so that you can better understand how you "vibrate" to the World around you, to your personal World and to its people and things.

| Destiny | Personality | Key impression | Ruling Planet |
|---|---|---|---|
| #1 | Pioneer | Leadership/ Independence | Sun |
| #2 | Helpmate | Understanding/ Adjustment | Moon |
| #3 | Artist | Expression/ Communication | Mercury |
| #4 | Builder | Discipline/ Organization | Earth |
| #5 | Adventurer | Freedom/ Movement | Mars |
| #6 | Harmonizer | Responsibility/ Healing | Venus |
| #7 | Mystic | Analysis/ Solitude | Saturn |
| #8 | Executive | Abundance/ Power | Jupiter |
| #9 | Metaphysician | Compassion/ Universality | Vulcan |
| #11 (20) | Visionary | Revelation/ Idealism | Neptune |
| #13 (4) | Chosen | Spiritual Mastery/ Able | Pluto |
| #22(4) | Genius | Material Mastery/ Realism | Uranus |

Pythagoras first identified the energy associated with each "vibrating number."

By assigning the proper value to each letter of your name, you can determine your own *Expression Number*. Your Expression number explains "how" you go about the business of your Life. When compared to the Destiny number, which is the value of your date of birth, the day, month, and year, when added together, you will have a much better understanding of who you are this time around, and how to enhance your Life accordingly.

Here is the Value-Chart for each letter of the alphabet, including the letters (sounds) which represent *Master Numbers*. If the "K," "M" or the "V" are in your name, understand that they call for only your best, most concentrated effort to live up to the special Qualities you're blessed with.

# Table of Letter Values

| 1 | 2 | 3 | 4 | 5 | 6 | 7 | 8 | 9 |
|---|---|---|---|---|---|---|---|---|
| A | B | C | D | E | F | G | H | I |
| J | K | L | M | N | O | P | Q | R |
| S | T | U | V | W | X | Y | Z | |

By assigning the proper number value to each letter of your name, you can determine your own *Expression Number*, which defines HOW you go about the business of your Life. Compare the *Expression* number and *Destiny Numbers* to make the most of the Life you've been given.

Always reduce the sum's total to a single digit, paying special attention to the *Master Numbers* since they indicate superior opportunities for growth and development. Again, the *Master Numbers* are "K" (2), "M" (4) and "V" (4).

For example, let's use the fictitious woman I referenced earlier:

Sally Marie Fletcher
7. 23. 1968
36/9

What do her *Expression Numbers* add up to? Practice with her name here and then move on to your own name. Does her name include any *Master Number/Letter vibrations?* What are they? Does your own name contain any combination of *Master Numbers* or *Letter vibrations*?

When Albert Einstein gave us his mathematical theories and his explanation of the order of the Universe, he spoke about Astrology and Numerology and the vibrations that are given out through numbers. The numbers form the basis of our Universe and explain the way the human psyche works. I'm with Dr. Einstein on this one.

## Action Steps

Once again, by hand, write this work out using the space provided here or in your own journal. As you delve deeper into the wonderful mystery that you are, you'll be even more eager to continue this journey toward the real *self*.

Have some fun with your own birthdate and those of close friends and family, and I'm willing to bet you'll find some common threads. Start with yourself ~ always ~ since understanding who we are and how we tick is the greatest surprise/magical mystery tour of them all. As you practice more, you'll discover what you appreciate and how you resonate with each number vibration. Then try to figure out the *whys* and the deeper meanings.

Physically write out your birthdate first, and then proceed to your full name at birth since that imprint stays with you throughout this Life experience. If you are married and took your husband's or your partner's last name, then include that in the mix and see how that new last name has affected or changed your Life story. Just as an aside, I always strongly urge women to *never* change their maiden name since that is the link to our Spiritual empowerment, and we should own it.

# Chapter Four

## Breath Work

If you're not breathing, nothing in your body is working. From that first *Breath of Life* we take to the last as we leave this Life, breath fuels everything. The average adult takes between 21,600 ~ 28,000 breaths per day. When we have a conscious connection to those breaths, we open to extraordinary possibilities including better health, the ability to sleep and the ability to function better in every way.

*Become the leader in your own Life ~ harness the Breath of Life and then breathe it into everything in front of you and thrive!*

Throughout history, breath and our connection to it have been the basis for many disciplines from every corner of the planet. Here are just a few to begin working with as you recognize the value of this discipline and incorporate mindful breathing into your own daily practice.

The following information comes from my work with Sufi Master Jabrane M. Sebnat.

**********************

## Take in and Blow Out

To take in and blow out, use your breath as a signal to the inner self to consciously "take in" an experience and to consciously "blow out" an experience. This is especially helpful when you're suddenly faced with an immediate unpleasant experience or any personal crisis. The method is fast, the process is effective, and your breath is always right there and available to you.

Simply inhale the "event/experience/fear" through the nose with all of your might and focus on it, then turn your head to the <u>right</u> and blow the air out through your mouth.

If you're left with the sense that you haven't finished, repeat the exercise with vigor! Repeat it once again if necessary, being mindful to not "hold on" to the experience. Let the breath, the experience, go.

This particular breathing exercise is fast, simple, and extremely effective in a variety of circumstances. Use it as often as necessary. The more you breathe, the healthier you will be.

## Huna Breath

Huna breath comes from the practical system of psychology long used by the *Kahuna* of ancient Hawaii. Through a process of *HA* or *Divine Breath*, one is prepared to do meditation, problem solving, counseling, healing, and self-introspection, which are vital when embarking on a course of deeper personal work. I always suggest inhaling through the nose and exhaling through the mouth, unless otherwise indicated.

Here is the process:

*Inhale* (Cosmic Energy) to the count of seven to energize every cell, tissue, blood vessel, muscle, bone, and atom in the whole body.

*Hold* the breath to the count of seven to allow the body to rest momentarily, thereby slowing down the metabolism, enriching the body chemistry, and regenerating the cells, etc. Above all, breath can prevent "shock" to the system while exchanging these two powerful forces of inhalation and exhalation.

*Exhale* (Cosmic Energy) to the count of seven as you exhale through the mouth. Deliberately releasing impurities, poisons, and blocks from the body system.

*Rest* for the count of seven. This is considered to be one round of breathing.

The entire process requires seven rounds of breathing. The process of "HA" is one of the oldest methods known for accumulating Mana or Vital Life Force Energy.

The Huna Breath is an excellent way to quickly charge the system with a jolt of energy, which can then be directed for sports, a specifically taxing work or personal situation, or to simply reenergize the body as a whole. Think of it as a "Breath of Life Tune-Up."

If you find that the count of seven breaths is too much for you, start with rounds of four breaths and then build up to five and then six, eventually becoming more comfortable with the actual Seven Rounds of Breathing. The next time you have a daunting task in front of you, give the *HA* breathing technique a try. I am quite sure you'll be amazed and delighted at what you're able to conjure within yourself. Although this process is most often connected to the healing art known as Huna, it has also been referred to as square breathing to those unfamiliar with the ancient practice.

## Walking Gently on This Earth

Walking gently on this Earth, is a breathing exercise to help us remember our home, "School House Planet Earth," and our ongoing commitment and connection to it.

Here is the process:

Stand up as you normally would. Begin to move around the room in your usual manner. After a moment or two of movement, come to a complete halt and begin to breathe deliberately and slowly into every cell in your physical body.

Continue breathing until your body begins to feel vitalized and fully alive. At this point, slowly extend your right foot up and outward, placing the foot gently on the surface of the floor or the ground. Stop there and breathe fully once again.

When you have reestablished yourself as consciously breathing into every cell of your body, take your second step by moving your left foot forward in the same way and placing it gently on the floor or the ground in front of you.

As you make these motions, become so silent that you imagine or feel yourself to be invisible. Each step, every single footprint, is meant to carry you forward with renewed consciousness while at the same time not harming the surface of Mother Earth.

Continue with this exercise until you have made your way around the entire room or the outside setting. As you finish, glance around at the area you've just covered and give a silent prayer of thanks. Remember, always, that we are visitors, guests, on Blessed Mother Earth.

\*\*\*\*\*\*\*\*\*\*\*\*\*\*\*\*\*\*\*\*\*\*\*\*

# Basic Balancing Breath

Basic balancing breath is a gentle breathing technique that can be incorporated at any time in your Spiritual Practice.

Here is the process:

Sitting in a comfortable position with your back straight and your feet on the floor, *inhale* through the nose to the count of four, imaging your entire body is breathing.

*Exhale* to the count of four, easily releasing anything that's ready to go.

*Hold* *empty* with no movement to the count of four.

Repeat the process four times in comfortable succession and notice how you feel after this easy exercise. Make a note in your journal of any emotions or sensations that may have risen to the surface.

# Action Steps

One by one, practice each breathing technique, observing how you feel. Be mindful of how the exercises affect your heart rate, mood, and physical sensations. Using the journal pages provided here or writing in your own journal, make note of your anxiety level, your level of skepticism, your pulse and even your blood pressure if that's an issue for you. Then write down your observations as clearly and succinctly as possible. You'll want to refer back to them as you progress over time. Your reactions and responses are bound to change.

*Take In and Blow Out the "Breath of Life":*
When could this technique help you? Think of a recent experience or something coming up that could happen soon when this particular breathing skill might be most helpful.

*Huna Breath:*
When could this technique help you? Think of a recent experience or something coming up that could happen soon when this particular breathing skill might be most helpful.

*Walking Gently on This Earth:*
When could this technique help you? Think of a recent experience or something coming up that could happen soon when this particular breathing skill might be most helpful.

*Basic Balancing Breath:*
When could this technique help you? Think of a recent experience or something coming up that could happen soon when this particular breathing skill might be most helpful.

There are countless breathing techniques and just as many theories to go with them. Your job is to discover what suits you best and then to deliberately include it in your daily practice. Work with a breath coach if necessary, and by all means, record your progress in this book in the journal pages provided or in your own journal for future reference. The breath and your connection to it are valuable for a productive, healthy, successful Life.

*Breath is the king of the mind.* ~ B.K.S. Iyengar

# Chapter Five

## Affirmations, Incantations and Mantras

Research has indicated that the average American has roughly 60,000 thoughts per day, and the majority of those lofty thoughts are the same ones we had the day before. If we're really stuck in a rut (and most of us are about one thing or another), chances are those are the same re- worked and re-processed thoughts we've been having for a while. With that in mind, I'm offering some important ways to shift thoughts with focus and determination. Once you have harnessed the power of your thoughts and expanded your sense of self to include new resources, the World you live in will be one of deliberate creation and not just happenstance. You will have the power to rise out of any rut.

Important tools to help you become the deliberate creator of your Life and to have the Life of your dreams are *Affirmations*, *Incantations* and *Mantras*.

The use of Affirmations has long been a powerful moment-by-moment method of training the mind to deliberately attract the best possible state of consciousness. When you believe that "like attracts like" and that we live in a World where the "Law of Attraction" is constantly in motion, creating and maintaining a better mindset set is possible.

To accomplish that, you must change your thinking first and foremost. If those thoughts that fuel your actions and responses to Life do not change, you are at the mercy of the ever-changing "tides of Life" and unable to access your own greatness. The World needs you whole, complete, and in your best state of mind. And you deserve to live a Life of greater joy, accomplishment, and ease.

An *Affirmation* is defined as any particular word or statement that helps us to shift our state of being, whether that's a particular new goal or a hoped-for change for the better. Ultimately, we can change in only one of three ways: what we **think**, what we **do,** and what we **believe**. Our beliefs are the toughest to shift and are almost always preceded by a deliberate and calculated desire to be or do better. Something must spark our imagination and our curiosity in order to motivate us to seek something new. Affirmations are a great place to start.

An Affirmation can be as simple as, "I can do better!" Here are a few favorite Affirmations that have worked for me for years. If these feel good to you, by all means, claim them for yourself.

Affirmations

I love you [insert your name]! I trust you [insert your name]! You matter to me [insert your name]!

I am safe with you [insert your name]! You're precious to me [insert your name]!

Continue as above, telling yourself that you are: beautiful ~ talented ~ creative ~ smart ~ capable and wise. If you have hesitation, that's normal. Keep up with these positive statements until resistance has been removed or you can at least laugh at yourself while in the process.

I AM a Being of Divine Light! I AM a Child of God! God knows and loves the real me!
I know I can change any of my circumstances for the better!
I deserve a happy Life!
I matter to the World; my presence is important to Life!
I AM trusting the process of Life!
I AM enough just as I AM, and I always have been!
I AM cared for, and others count on me!
I deserve every good thing Life has to offer!
I AM the best expression of Life that I can be in this moment!
I AM open and receptive to change!
My good is everywhere, and I AM open to finding it, easily!
All I need to know will be revealed to me!
I am a part of the Divine plan of Life!
Today is the best day of my Life, and I know it!!

Here is an Affirmation I have used for years, having always attributed it to Stuart Wilde, the famous British author and New Age Spiritual teacher. However, I can find no trace of it in any of his books, and I now believe I got this from his cassette series, "Your Infinite Self," which I listened to on repeat for many years in the 1990s. If this does not come from Stuart Wilde, my deep thanks to whomever wrote these inspiring words:

*I am happy, healthy, prosperous and successful. The Infinite Intelligence of my subconscious mind aids me and guides me in every endeavor. All obstacles to my progress have been removed. I rest in a sea of Universal love, understanding, oneness, and Light. I am a part of that Light. I am one with that Light. I am indeed that LIGHT!*

Try setting the tone for the day with this:

*Today is a day of completion; I give thanks for this perfect day, miracles shall follow miracles and wonders shall never cease.* ~ Florence Scovel Shinn

Feel free to create your own Affirmations to suit your needs, keeping them centered on the "I AM" principle at all times.

You'll find action steps and suggestions at the end of this chapter.

## Incantations

An *Incantation* is usually defined as having a mystical connection to charms, enchantments and a true burst of power. Think of an Incantation as a magical formula intended to create a specific desired effect on another person or situation. The word incantation comes from the Latin word *incantare*, meaning *to enchant*. As with any mystical tool of empowerment, we must never wish ill will on another. Instead, intentionally focus on the highest and the best outcome for yourself and for all those you come in contact with. Remember, we are all Divinely connected.

The "I AM Incantations" which I am quoting here are said to have been handed down through the ages from Saint Germain. Said to be the Master of the 7th Ray, which is the Ray of Transmutation, Saint Germain is a Master Alchemist of the sacred Fire, offering us the gift of the Violet Flame of freedom for World transmutation. I have always had a special affinity for these, and I use these Incantations daily. Again, this is one of those many situations where I have had the material for so long that I have no memory of the origin or my source of learning.

When I repeat these, I am always left with a feeling of peaceful grace and the awareness that I have righted any wrongs I may have sent out into the Universe.

If these resonate with you, then, by all means, use them as a way to deepen your personal connection to God and to strengthen your relationship to the right action as it moves through you.

I AM Incantations

I, _____, do hereby withdraw all power, which I have given to other people or to situations to control my experience in all areas of my Life. I am a victim no longer! I am in control of my experiences and by knowing this and choosing this, I start myself on the road to perfect peace and joyous fulfillment in all areas of my Life.

I AM the open door, which no man can shut, into the great opulence of GOD waiting, surging to press forward to heal, to Bless and to prosper me abundantly.

Mighty I AM presence, go forth into my business World and consume everything unlike THY mighty self and replace all with the mighty perfection of GOD ~ which I AM!

I AM the mighty consuming flame that now and forever consumes all past and present mistakes, their cause and their effect, and all undesirable creations for which my outer self is responsible.

I AM the power of my complete self-control forever sustained.

I AM the presence pouring into this condition, solving it for me right now. I AM harmonious. I AM peaceful. I AM alert to the direction of my GOD-self as it flows through me.

Beloved I AM Presence, seize my power of qualification. Let me qualify all things with only LIGHT and LOVE.

I AM the visible presence of those greatly beloved Ascended Masters whom I wish to have appear here with me, and whose assistance I desire now and always.

I AM the only presence acting in this. I AM the only presence acting in my World.

Thank you GOD, Thank you GOD, Thank you GOD!

I will to will THY will, and it is done!

If these Incantations spark something within you to search deeper, please continue research on "Ascended Masters" for a deeper look at all of those who are always waiting to help us. If one Ascended Master in particular pulls at you, then claim that one for yourself and dig even deeper into that Master's origin and particular power, gifts and grace.

It may also prove helpful to you if you search out "Decrees," which have long been used to command action on one's behalf. If this interests you, please Google: "Beloved Great Soul Beings" and see what you might find.

## Mantras

Mantram or Personal Mantram or Mantra as tools of spiritual significance are nothing new to people from India or other ancient cultures. In our Western culture, with our Judeo-Christian focus, using a Mantra can seem peculiar or awkward at best.

The earliest known Mantras were composed in Vedic Sanskrit in India. Long believed to be the first sound which originated on Earth, is the simple yet profound, AUM or OM. If reading about this work is sparking an internal interest in you right now, please search out the Vedic Sutras and prepare to be amazed. Giving yourself plenty of time to digest the information.

It is said that if a person only uttered the "**OM**" Mantra, that would be quite enough to put one on a better course for their future growth. I will give more examples of how to incorporate the "**OM**" as we go along here.

Throughout the ages, every major religion has used a Mantram, and most often, more than one. Since I was raised as an Irish Catholic, the "Hail Mary," when used in reference to the Blessed Mother, has always been close to my heart. In fact, when I am in any kind of jeopardy, it's the first thing that comes to mind for me. It's so automatic that I often find myself repeating it over and over until any sense of unrest has passed.

The "Ava Maria" is also a traditional Catholic Mantra, and if it feels good to you, claim it as your own.

In India, one of the oldest and best-known Mantras is "Rama" and translates to one of the names of the Lord that comes from a word meaning "joy" or even "to rejoice." Hence, the use of "Rama, Rama, Rama" is to be calling on the source of joy within our own hearts.

Here are some seed Mantras, their pronunciation, and the principles behind them:

| Seed Mantra | Pronunciation | Principle |
| --- | --- | --- |
| Shrim | Shreem | Abundance/Feminine |
| Klim | Kleem | Attraction |
| Dum | Doom | Protection/Feminine |
| Krim | Kreem | Burn Away/Feminine |
| Gum | Just like chewing Gum. | Remove Obstacles |

Here are some examples of these Seed Mantras and their applications: Using Shrim and Klim together:

"OM Shrim Klim, Lakshmi, Svaha!" which is specifically to be used by a woman to create a greater sense of abundance in all areas of their lives. The closing of this Mantra, "Svaha" is feminine in nature.

"OM Gum, Ganepatia, Namaha!" which is a Mantra to the Ganehsa, the oldest son of Shiva and his wife, Parvati. This is the Mantra to use when you want an immediate miracle and the removal of anything blocking your good. The closing of this Mantra, "Namaha" is masculine in nature.

Other similar examples include these:

"OM Nama Shiva, OM Nama Shiva, OM Nama Shiva (continue to repeat as often as feels right to you). The translation is "OM, I surrender to the Divine," or, "May the Elements of this creation abide in me in perfection."

"OM Mani Padme Hum," which is a Tibetan Buddhist Mantra to the Bodhisattva of Compassion, Avalokiteshwara. The translation is, "The jewel of the mind has reached the heart's lotus," since when the mind and the heart are in unison, anything can happen. This has long been considered to be the Mantra of personal transformation.

Shifting gears just a bit now, I've felt a kinship with Judaism my whole Life, and I used to attend Synagogue with a special friend in my childhood. It was quite an astonishing moment for me the first time incense was used at Temple, and it was the same incense used in the High Holy Masses at my Catholic Church. It hit me then that perhaps we are all more alike than we are different!

My favorite Jewish Mantra *Barukh Attah Adonai* means *Blessed art thou, O Lord* in English. The first time I heard it chanted, my heart expanded, and I felt "whole," as if something was being reawakened in the annals of my personal Karmic history. As with any Mantra, be alert to that immediate sense of connection. The sense of empowerment will increase with repetition, so once you've chosen a Mantra, repeat it as often as possible.

As I said at the start of this section, our Western mindset it quite different than those of older cultures, so approach this with a sense of ease. Don't be tempted to jump around or to create your own Mantra, instead relying on Mantras of tradition. For example, my personal Mantra, which was privately given to me by one of my teachers in 2003, is one that I still work with today. I use all of those mentioned above, but I always revert to the one closest to my heart. It not only soothes me, but it conjures up the now physically departed essence of my beloved teacher, Bea Scarlata.

I believe one of the most important Mantras ever created was written by Alice A. Bailey. Born in England and raised in North America, Alice A. Bailey was one of the first Spiritual teachers to use the term, "New Age" in her classes and writing. While many are familiar with the last stanza, known as "The Great Invocation," all three stanzas were written in response to the growing world tensions in the 1930s and 1940s.

## The Solar Mantram

I.     "Let the forces of Light bring illumination to mankind. Let the Spirit of Peace be abroad. May men of goodwill everywhere join in the spirit of cooperation. Let the Spirit of forgiveness be invoked by men everywhere ~ one toward the other. Let Power attend the efforts of the great servers of humanity." (Stanza One, written in 1935)

II.     "Let the Lords of Liberation issue forth. Let them bring succor to the Sons of Men. Let the Rider from the secret place come forth, and coming, save. Come forth, Oh Mighty One! Let the Souls of men awaken to the Light, and may they stand with massed intent. Let the fiat of the Lord go forth ~ the end of woe has come. Come forth, Oh Mighty One!. The hour of service of the saving force has now arrived. Let it be spread abroad, Oh Mighty Lord! Let Light and Love, and Power and Death, fulfill the purpose of the Coming One. Come forth, Oh Mighty One! The will to save is here. The Love to carry on the work is wide abroad. The active aid of all who know the Truth is also here. Come forth, Oh Mighty One, and blend these three. Construct a great defending wall; the rule of evil now must end. Come forth, Oh Mighty One." (Stanza Two, written in 1940)

## The Great Invocation

III.     From the point of Light within the Mind of God, let Light stream forth into the minds of men. Let Light descend on Earth. From the point of Love within the Heart of God, let love stream forth into the hearts of men. May Christ return to Earth. From the centre where the Will of God is known, let purpose guide the little wills of men ~ the purpose which the Masters know and serve. From the centre which we call the race of men, let the Plan of Love and Light work out, and may it seal the door where evil dwells. Let Light and Love and Power restore the plan on Earth." (Stanza Three, written in 1945)

This entire Mantra stirred deep feelings and a genuine desire to be better and do better with my Life as an offering to God and the Holy Spirit. If it speaks to you, by all means, claim it for yourself. The Solar Mantram was written in three stages over the course of ten or twelve years, depending on what source you reference. Author Alice A. Bailey who was also an esteemed Theosophical teacher. She wrote more than twenty-four books throughout her lifetime. At the age of fifteen, she was visited by the "essence of a tall stranger dressed in European clothes and wearing a turban who told her she needed to develop self-control in preparation for the work he planned for her to do." Her "Master of Wisdom," also referred to as *DK* or *Djwal Khul*, was the Spiritual entity that channeled information through her for nineteen of her most influential books. In 1922 she and her husband, Foster Bailey, founded The Lucis Trust to fund and administer activities devoted to "right human relations." Over the last forty years, these Mantras have been "updated" to suit current "trends" of the day. However, I am never one to "update" sacred materials, and I am using the same work I was first given in 1983. By all means, if you're curious, search out the updated versions for yourself by visiting the Lucis Trust at lucistrust.org.

## Mantras That Speak To Me

Affirmations, Incantations, and Mantras may not seem to be that special, but they are magnificent, age-old tools for centering yourself and for moving into a deeper, more meaningful internal dialogue with yourself. They are meant to move you toward a more reverent awareness of the many privileges we are all afforded simply by being alive.

Approach this work with intention, spending time with yourself as you dig deeper into your own sense of meaning and value. And as always, write these out in long hand in the pages here or in a journal to receive the best benefits available to you. Life is a miraculous journey, and as I have discovered time and time again, magic and untold wonders are at every turn. The more curious and eager we are to learn, the better we are for it.

## Action Steps

Using the journal pages provided here or working in your own journal, write out by hand what your favorite Affirmation, Incantation or Mantra might be.

Slowly and with intention, go back and re-read all of this chapter, paying close attention to any sensations you might feel of energy moving through your body. Notice what piques your curiosity and follow that path to see where it might lead you.

Sit with it quietly and literally "take in" the words and the essence. If something in particular speaks to you, write it out over and over again until you feel you have taken it directly into your heart and consciousness.

Spend time then writing out your own personal Affirmations and revisit them daily for the next twenty-one days ~ morning and night. I promise you that your Life will shift in extraordinary ways. Prepare to be astonished at how your personal point of attraction for good things has grown exponentially.

# Chapter Six

## The Angelic Kingdom

If you've ever been the recipient of a true miracle, then you've been touched by this extraordinary realm of magnificent beings. Throughout history, every major religion and culture has spoken of the existence of supernatural beings. To the uninitiated, these extraordinary beings from realms of super-physical consciousness may seem to be nonsense. If you happen to fall into that category, please suspend your negative inner talk about the subject and allow your own Deep Internal Body Wisdom to kick in. You can always go "back there" if you are more comfortable in that arena, but my sense is that being open to new concepts and fresh ideas keeps us in the healthy flow of Life. Please give it a try and join me there.

I believe that we live in a physical realm surrounded by tens of thousands of Angelic Beings whose only task is to keep us alive and relatively safe. I also believe in the existence of personal Guardian Angels who have been with us since the beginnings of our journeys into physical form.

Much like the famous Catholic print of a Guardian Angel shepherding young children across the creek, Guardian Angels are always with us, doing their best to help and to guide us accordingly.

My personal Guardian Angel was introduced to me a number of years ago by a gifted Angelic Healer. This healer, with extraordinary etheric vision, was able to discover and to name my Guardian Angel. Her name is BETTY, and much as I argued with the name ~ I tried to "fancy it up" by spelling it "Bette," my healing consultant would have none of it.

My Betty is a tall, perpetually youthful being with blondish-red hair that falls to her shoulders in a cascade of curls. She's dressed in long flowing robes of pink with touches of lace and golden threads throughout. I was told that she is patient (she'd have to be), with an excellent sense of humor, and that she is kind. During that first virtual consultation, the back of my neck began to tingle with awareness as I gazed around my office at the various replicas of Angels dressed in similar fashion. From the tiny ceramic Angel, kneeling in prayer and dressed in a pink gown with golden wings, that I always keep on top of my scheduling book, to the tall and regal wooden Angel that was hand made for me, also dressed in a gown of gold and pink with curly reddish blonde hair. They both appeared to be smiling at me with twinkles in their eyes at my sudden, yet shocking, newfound awareness. Betty replicas had been watching over me all along.

What are the odds of that happening? Even the Christmas Angel who has graced the top of my Christmas tree for many years is an exact replica of my personal Guardian Angel. I remember when that gift was first given to me, when I bristled a bit inside at the notion that a Christmas tree topper would be dressed in pink and gold. Since that fateful consultation with my Angelic Healer years ago, I've laughed at that many times since. How little we mortals know! When I continued to protest to my Angelic consultant that I simply could not have a Guardian Angel named Betty since my first husband's ex-wife had been named Betty, and she made my Life a "living hell," Lindy's comment was simply that "God has an excellent sense of humor and perhaps I should develop one as well"! Over the years, I have made a concerted effort to not only make friends with Betty and to lean on her, consult with her, and call on her daily for guidance. And guess what? The more I have learned to trust Betty's presence in my Life, the better my Life has gotten. To say that Betty and I are tight would be an understatement, and yes, I do hear her routinely laughing at me in equal proportion to her nurturing hugs.

Angels are pure beings of Divine Light who are sent to us by God. These Angelic Beings are not to be feared or avoided but instead should be invited into the everyday happenings of our lives to make things better. Their love for us is unconditional. They see only the best of who we are inside, and they encourage us onward no matter what's going on.

I believe we all have a natural affinity for certain Angelic Beings. In my personal case, I have always had a deep affection and closeness with Jesus and Lord Michael the Arch Angel. At the moment of my birth, both of these Divine entities appeared at the foot of my mother's bed, assuring her that we would both live through what was proving to be a precarious trial of birth.

In addition to Jesus and Lord Michael, I have always been drawn to Saint Germain and Archangels Raphael, Uriel, and Gabriel. If you do not feel a special affinity for any one of these Angelic beings, do some research of your own. As you do, pay particular attention to your internal responses and changes in your body temperature, which might be alerting you to a special affinity. However, if you simply allow Google to be your friend and search, "Angels," you'll be directed to the Los Angeles Angels baseball team. A much better bet would be to search the term, "Angelic Beings," which will provide you with a good overview of The Angelic Realm. For those of you who are drawn to Angelic work, I would recommend *The Angelic Kingdom*, compiled from the teachings of the *Bridge to Freedom* by Werner Schroeder. This is available through the Ascended Masters Teaching Foundation in Mount Shasta, California. A treasure trove of practical guidance and healing, it is dedicated "in love and gratitude to the Seven Mighty Archangels who represent the Divine feeling nature of God."

Angels are supernatural beings or Spirits in certain religions and mythologies, with over 250 mentions of Angels in Scripture from Genesis to Revelation. As we are reminded in Hebrews 13:2, "Do not forget to entertain strangers, for by so doing some have unwittingly entertained Angels." (New King James Version)

The three major religions of the Western World—Christianity, Judaism and Islam—all include Angels in their various cosmologies. It is commonly accepted in Christian belief that Angels are organized into three hierarchies and nine orders or choirs so that the Angels can be classified and ranked.

The First hierarchy contains Seraphim, Cherubim and Thrones. The Second hierarchy contains Dominions, Virtues and Powers and The Third hierarchy contains Principalities, Archangels and Angels.

One of my most treasured books says this in the introduction: "One of the most Blessed realizations that can come to any man is the one which enables him to know of the countless lives that exist about him invisible to his outer senses. Human beings are but a single manifestation of the Infinite Creator. Besides them are hosts of Ascending Forms intent upon final unification within the spirit of the Eternal Maker." The name of the book is *Natives of Eternity*, and it was written by Flower Newhouse in 1944 and published by J.F. Rowny Press, Santa Barbara, California. Said to be an "authentic record of experiences in realms of Super-physical

Consciousness," it contains a number of exquisite paintings by Mildred Compton. The many idealistic conceptions of Angels include, "An Angel of The Morning," "An Angel of Birth," and "An Angel of Music," to name just a few of these captivating depictions of Angelic Beings.

The presence of Angels as historical beings has been documented in fine art throughout the ages. The *Three Archangels with Tobias* by Frances Botticini (1471) is a lovely depiction of Archangels Michael, Raphael and Gabriel coming to the aid of a young man. The mythical and the Life of imagination come alive in Gustave Moreau's "Voices of Evening" (1885) offering another glimpse of three Angels at work.

The number three is an important, recurring number throughout Christianity. The Holy Family was visited by Three Kings, Jesus arose from the dead after three days. The Godhead itself consists of three persons. We also know from the study of Numerology that the number three is ruled by the Planet Mercury and governs communication in all forms, including Angelic communications to those of us on the Earth Plane.

If you feel so inclined, please do your own Angelic research, remaining open to all of the magic that surrounds you, and using any of the resources I've mentioned. You can even start your own investigation tonight by "inviting in" the presence of your own Guardian Angel by asking them to visit you during sleep. By consciously opening the door to this lovely personal connection, your Life will be enriched in countless ways. Keep a notepad next to the bed to record any sensations, memories or ideas that may come to you in the dream state. Good luck, and enjoy the magic as it unfolds.

Noted author, Marianne Williamson says this about Angels: "We must learn to think only Divine thoughts. Angels are the thoughts of GOD, and in Heaven, humans think like Angels. Angels light the way."

## Action Steps

Using the journal pages provided here or working in your own journal, sit quietly for a few moments and invite your inner self to consciously remember encounters you may have had with Angels.

Recall frightening times, hopeless moments and even near misses that threatened your Life. Just maybe an Angel came to your aid.

If you're feeling particularly inspired, allow your hand to simply begin writing without your conscious intent and see what happens.

Keep writing and inviting your Angels to reveal themselves to you now.

# Chapter Seven

## Devas, Faeries and The Illumined Ones

Following our discussion of the Angelic Realm and how these Divine Beings could be a resource of ongoing comfort and endless enhancement to your Life, I would like to introduce you to another realm of magnificent, elevated beings known as Devas.

## Devas

In her book, *Map: The Co-Creative White Brotherhood Medical Assistance Program*, Machelle Small Wright says *Deva* and *nature spirits* are "names used to identify two different levels and functions within the nature consciousness. They are two levels within the larger nature consciousness that interface with the human Soul while in form."

As such, Devas belong to a group of Earth Elementals, the Spirits most closely associated with specific aspects of Nature. If this piques your curiosity, it would be a fascinating study to research "The Tibetan Wheel of Life" which refers to Devas as being in the "Realm of the Gods." You can find these references online quite easily.

Throughout recorded history, Devas can be found in Buddhist cosmology, in Chinese, Japanese, and of course, in Sanskrit writings from India as well.

Said to occupy the realms of infinite space and infinite consciousness, nothingness and *everythingness* all at once, Devas are not omniscient or omnipotent creatures but very powerful beings whose lives span countless ages. A Deva's body is much larger than that of humans and shines with a brilliant light illuminating their exquisite beingness, perhaps offering us a not so gentle hint of their magical powers and supernatural senses; we are powerless to hide anything from them, nor should we try.

Their goal is to be of assistance to our Earth, creating a cohesive framework within which humanity is able to function. Just think of all the structures or frameworks we have in place to keep society as we know it functioning: religious movements, educational movements, governmental constructs, the arts of science, medicine, philosophy and even the flow and the structure of our everyday movements through our lives. All of these operate thanks to the patience, the wisdom and the grace of the Devas watching over us all.

The Devas I am most closely associated with come from my study and daily interaction with *MAP: The Co-Creative White Brotherhood Medical Assistance Program*, as mentioned earlier, written and researched by the incomparable Machelle Small Wright. In Machelle's ongoing work with Earth Elementals at her Perelandra Center for Nature Research in Virginia, she was taken on a journey into a deeper level of experience than even she knew existed. Her patience, curiosity, and scientific brain have given us a superb vehicle for our personal ongoing healing and deeper exploration of all that God has afforded us on this most curious path through Life.

In the introduction to this book, written in 1990 by Dr. Albert Schatz, Ph.D., he states, "I am convinced that our only salvation is what Machelle Small Wright calls 'co-creative science.' This involves our conscious establishment, a co-creative partnership with Nature. Co- creative science is qualitatively different from the science we know because it integrates the revolutionary dynamic of nature (order, organization, and Life vitality/action) with the evolutionary dynamic of man (definition, direction, and purpose). Machelle's co-creative research with Nature is not only the light at the end of the tunnel. It is also the entrance to the tunnel and the tunnel itself."

I have had the privilege of doing MAP work for myself since 1992, when a friend gave me the first edition of this remarkable work as a gift. I urge you to do your own research as a Life-enriching gift to yourself. Please do not be put off by the name White Brotherhood, as it has nothing to do with any white supremacist group or sexist organization. These are beings of clear intent, including males, females, and Souls beyond either persuasion, and they appear in a stunning array of colorful patterns. The name "White Brotherhood" is one that has been used for centuries by this group of extraordinary beings whose only intention is to be of service to humanity. When I open my own MAP session, I always ask to be connected with my personal MAP team, I refer to my White Brotherhood Unit as such. I also refer to them as the "Illumined Ones" which fills me with a profound sense of lightness and connectedness.

You can find Machelle Small Wright through her website: www.perelandra-ltd.com to investigate the brilliant work she is doing in the world and to access a full list of her books.

A study of the Six Realms of Existence under the heading of "Buddhist Teachings" on the Internet provides an in-depth look at the complexities of the DEVAS, which is not only fascinating to me but quite intimidating and awe inspiring all at once. I realize more every day all I do not know ~ yet!

# Action Steps

Using the journal pages provided here or working in your own journal, sit quietly as you reflect on what you have just read as you invite your inner self to consciously remember any encounters you may have had with Devas.

Have you ever been working in the garden and felt the presence of unseen visitors?

Or perhaps you've been walking on a nature trail for the first time while feeling or sensing the presence of visitors not easily seen by the naked eye. Write about those experiences.

# Faeries

'Tis true, well before Walt Disney first introduced the World to Tinker Bell in 1953, famed British author J.M. Barrie had created the character of Tinker Bell in his 1904 novel: *Peter Pan*. Suddenly the World of fairies or faeries became more accessible to ordinary folks like you and me. J.M. Barrie had a whimsical way of introducing us to an intricate and frequently underestimated community of diverse beings.

The words *fey* and *faerie* are French in origin and came into common usage during the Tudor period as replacements for the Old English references to *elf*. Shakespeare was the first to popularize this change of reference, although *Elfland*, *Faerieland*, *Elf* and *Faerie* are still considered to be interchangeable.

Fairy or Fairies refers to a particular, sweet, diminutive female species of Elementals who usually come to us with no ill intent.

That cannot be said for all of the diverse species of Elementals found in this unique and mysterious culture. Much as humans like to think of ourselves as a "superior" species, the realm of Fairies represents a level of magical ability and sheer empowerment that is incomprehensible to humans. We trifle with them at our own peril.

Anyone who has spent considerable time in Nature has had contact with the Land of Faeries. Whether you're an amateur gardener or a seasoned farmer, at some point you have had a mystical encounter with a Nature Spirit. Beware the person who is aware of this Kingdom and does not first ask the dirt for permission to dig. The law is that if you know about these extraordinary realms of DEVAS and FAERIES, you must first ask their permission or risk a bout of Poison Ivy and or a dead garden, ruined crops, or worse.

Included in the realm of Faeries are all sorts of fascinating creatures, including Dwarfs, Pixies, Selkies, Elves, and Mermaids. Goblins are also included and represent a breed of rather small, swarthy, and occasionally malicious beings who enjoy tempting humans who are unschooled in the finer arts of "Faerieland."

An excellent example of the intricate World of goblins is found in the works of J.K. Rowling throughout the Harry Potter series of books. The goblins are the ones who are tasked with guarding and running Gringotts Wizarding Bank, the wizarding World's premier financial institution. Griphook, a primary goblin, is said to be quite loyal to Gringotts as he oversees a workforce of equally shrewd and cunning goblin workers. Said to be naturally distrustful of humans, goblins are skilled craftsmen, especially when crafting swords and other magical items from metal. All of the traits used by the author are mentioned in various reference books I've studied over the years. I am deeply impressed and rather in awe of the research J.K. Rowling did while writing the Harry Potter books. If you're not a Harry Potter fan, please consider becoming one at once. It introduces us to so many levels of consciousness, good and bad behavior, and the brilliant possibilities afforded to us all when we learn to dream and use our magic for good.

Another group of Faerie creatures included in the Harry Potter cast of characters are Elves, most notably Dobby the house-elf originally owned by the Malfoy family, and ultimately, a devoted rescuer to Harry and his friends. Dobby demonstrated the unique set of values and codes of conduct associated with this realm of creatures. Possessing super-human powers of intuition, an Elf waits, watches, misses nothing and is deeply attuned to any hint of bad behavior on the part of humans. Said to possess a unique temperament, an Elf lives by their own sense of inner direction, either coming to the aid of a human, or simply watching with detached bemusement as an uninformed human falls off the edge of their life.

Said to be supernatural beings, Elves were first referenced in Old English and Norse texts, and they played prominent roles in many Scottish, Welch, Irish and Scandinavian folklore. After studying this subject at length, I believe most, if not all, of the ancient civilizations have their own versions of Faeries, Elves, and other assorted mystical beings.

Shakespeare's Puck in *A Midsummer Night's Dream* is the perfect example of a naughty shape-shifting hobgoblin. Typical of the Elf/Faerie personality, Puck is the closest thing the play has to a protagonist. With a mischievous spirit, Puck seems to be the responsible party for all of the chaos, mishaps and complications suffered by the main characters.

Ireland has long given us the feisty Leprechauns, said to wear a 3-sided hat to use as an axis to spin feverishly upside down when the mood suddenly strikes them to be playful. Tricky, merry, and mischievous, Leprechauns take a special delight in teasing humans. My Irish grandmother, Margaret Mary Sherlock Cathcart, took great pride in telling anyone who would listen that the "Wee People" whom she had "heard" for her whole Life were the source of her astonishing psychic abilities. At my age of six or seven, when I told her I did the same thing she did when I talked to dead people, she gave me one horrified and startled look and said with great emphasis, "Jesus, Mary, and Joseph ~ I do not! I only talk to the Wee People!" I don't think we ever had another conversation after that. It was a very long time before I ever told anyone else that I could see, let alone talk with dead people.

J.R.R. Tolkien's *The Lord of The Rings* is a literal treasure trove of mystical beings. Told as a fantastical tale, this is a journey of reluctant heroes who set out to save the World from consummate evil. Drawn from Tolkien's extensive knowledge of philosophy and folklore, we are taken on an epic quest to middle-earth. Please indulge your senses and read this wonderful work, as it will help to expand your mind and give you a more thorough understanding of this lovely realm of Devas, Faeries, and Illuminated Ones.

## Illumined Ones

As I mentioned earlier, when I open and close each MAP Coning, I take a moment to call on my own MAP Team, referred to as my White Brotherhood Medical Unit. They are also referred to as Illuminated Ones, and I include this special, and I feel elevated name for these important beings, each time.

As I was writing this chapter, which shockingly took me over two weeks to gather my thoughts about, I had a wonderful realization. It could be completely wrong or wildly off base, but it's my truth at the moment so I'll share it with you.

I believe many of these extraordinary beings that I've been writing about here share the same illuminated being stature, and I know many have been with me always.

If a Divine Being from a realm of consciousness I have not been aware of before takes the time and makes the effort to come to my aid, what an astonishing gift that is.

Before I even knew of the Illumined Ones, and long before Machelle Small Wright began writing about them, I was the beneficiary of their loving care and Divine

Light. Let me explain a bit about my childhood as it's rather like a circular crossword puzzle through a fascinating garden of magical happenings.

As a child, it was quite common apparently for "strange things" to happen to me and around me. Many of these unusual situations included sparkling lights and very faint images of light-filled beings floating around me and above my bed. My mother was the only one who seemed interested in these oddities. She began studying Astrology when I was seven years old. Apparently, she thought understanding my Astrological chart might give her some insight into who this child was she had given birth to. It was a gift to me, and a skill I have relied on to this day.

Throughout my childhood I would catch glimpses of things "off in the shadows or to the side of my vision" and I just came to accept it as my "normal." The only time any actual "people images" appeared to me was about a year or so before I started kindergarten, when I routinely entertained a group of magical friends for tea and pretend cookies.

An old, wingback chair was in the corner of the living room, under the front windows. I held pretend tea parties for a rotating group of "friends" from all over the World in my sacred, safe space. There was an American Indian Princess (my word, Princess) and a young boy from India, or perhaps he was an Arab, and another young boy from Mexico who came to visit ever so often, and a black boy who didn't say much. Still, he had penetrating, dark, sad eyes that held so many secrets. There was also a beautiful, delicate little girl with reddish hair and porcelain skin who seemed "other Worldly." I think she came from Sweden or perhaps Denmark, she always wore a pinafore dress with lots of lace and sparkles. No matter what language was spoken, I always knew exactly what my special friends were saying to me. It was so nice to have friends.

After each tea party, I always told my mother who had been there and what we talked about - mind you, everyone presented as a four or five- year-old child, so the discussions weren't deep. But we did talk about community and neighborhood things like children do with their friends. After a while, my mother began to keep a journal of these gatherings in an old-fashioned "Schooltime Composition" book. It really got her attention when certain things I told her about my friend's lives began showing up on the nightly news. She then started quizzing me more intently about "what did they say, exactly" Rosemary?

Apparently, this was no ordinary group of "imaginary friends" as reports about earthquakes, political takeovers, and volcanic eruptions began to coincide with my pretend tea parties (without cookies).

The visits ended when I started school, and even though I most likely have had visitations from these ILLUMINED ONES over the years, our time as children had come to an end.

As for that notebook my mother meticulously kept, it was thrown out by an older sister. My mother passed away suddenly when I was just nineteen years old while I was living at college. In my family, once you were not on the premises, all bets were off regarding personal belongings, no matter how special they might have been.

Throughout the years, no matter who I was living with or where I was living, I was always mildly aware that I was not alone and that special beings were watching over me. But to me it was just "my normal" – kind of like not having to discuss the color of your eyes or your hair.

In my early twenties, I was close friends with and an occasional lover to a brilliant radio/TV talent in WPB, Fla. David lived in the cottage behind my shotgun apartment on Broadway. He was suffering from either flu or pneumonia, and I brought him to my apartment to nurse him back to health. As is typical in those shotgun apartments, you have to go through every room to get to the next. I had David strategically placed on the couch in the living room which was in a direct line of sight to my bedroom. I kept the door open so I could hear him if he called out to me in the night. But I slept like a rock, as they say, and I was happy to see David in much better shape the next morning. All of those "meds" and other concoctions I had tossed down his throat had apparently done their job.

As we were chatting over eggs and morning coffee, he started quizzing me about my nighttime "friends." Finally, he just got annoyed with me and said when he woke up and started to get up to use the bathroom, which he had to walk through my room to get to, he saw me surrounded by three enormous "blue people," at least twelve to fourteen feet tall. At first, he thought it was his fever, but the closer he looked, the more he realized he was seeing a true thing. When he started to get off the couch for a closer look, the BLUE BEING closest to the door apparently gave him a strong side eye while nodding his head "NO" and he wisely thought otherwise about intruding. As I type these words, I can see those strong eyes penetrating completely through David as if he were nothing more than a mere vapor. He was not allowed to invade that sacred space, no matter what his current relationship with me was. This was private and for my benefit, exclusively.

I clearly remember sitting at the tiny counter in my kitchen, feeling all warm and tingly inside as if I was "remembering" or "acknowledging" something that had always been with me, my private secret, but now my cover was totally blown. I told David, "Yes, they've always been with me, and they keep me safe." I think I was telling myself this as I was telling him, too. Although we remained close friends and work colleagues for years, we never spoke about the BLUE PEOPLE again. And to my knowledge he never shared the encounter with anyone else, either. My Blue People are definitely in the category of Illumined Beings.

I know now after years of study and research that these lovely beings are a part of my MAP Team, and they were protecting me and guiding me long before I knew of their existence. It's caused me to be more open minded and so endlessly curious about what else I might not know just yet. Countless wonders, I am quite sure.

Hopefully, I have opened you to a new world of wonders and exciting things to explore and to ponder. I realize we covered Angels in Chapter Six, and I mentioned this work previously, but I think it is important to mention once again. It is the "The Angelic Kingdom" compiled from the Teachings of the "Bridge to Freedom" by Werner Schroeder. You can find this through the Ascended Master Teaching Foundation in Mount Shasta, California. It is 447 pages in length, so accessing it online might be easier than printing off the entire document. To me this is a treasure trove of Biblical insight and guidance, along with a complete guide to the workings of the Archangels and various Ascended Masters. As with anything I might present to you, always check your own heart and your Deep Internal Body Wisdom to decide if something is for you or not.

# Action Steps

Using the journal pages provided here or working in your own journal, sit quietly for a few moments as you bring to mind any encounters you may have had with the realm of Fairies or Illumined Ones.

# Chapter Eight

## Intentional Direction of Energy

Everything in life involves the movement of energy, including every thought and every emotion we experience. We can optimize each moment of our lives by learning how to manage, direct and simply acknowledge just how powerful we are as Spiritual Beings having a Human Experience ~ if and when we learn to pay attention. When we recognize the power of each thought and then combine it with an understanding of how energy moves, we become more effective in every area of our lives. It takes great skill to become a good manager of our own mind/brain/emotional systems, but when it is deliberately attended to, we then have the best chance at becoming people of considerable depth, wisdom, and power. For many years I thought *power* was a bad thing and I did not deserve it. Then I realized I was simply afraid of my own power and equally unsure of how to unlock it and then to direct it appropriately. I am eternally grateful that I have lived long enough to wrap my head and my heart around a greater sense of myself and my place in the World.

As a recovering alcoholic, raised in a home with an alcoholic father who let temper fuel his every move, controlling my own emotions and temper were an all too present, moment-by-moment concern. I had to learn to manage my emotions and to make peace with my temper. Perhaps you are dealing with similar issues. Go easy on yourself and trust the process.

Everything in this book is meant to help you, so please keep stretching and expanding your ideas about everything. Most especially who you are and what you're capable of.

There is no such thing as a "private thought." If you've conjured it up in your mind/brain system and spent more than a few seconds mulling it over, that thought has left you and found its way out into the Universe, with or without your permission. And that my friends can be quite daunting to even think about. Pun absolutely intended.

*Energy cannot be created or destroyed, it can only be changed from one form to another.* ~ Albert Einstein, Mathematician and Theoretical Physicist

If you were sitting in my office or we were meeting virtually, I would use the example that we as human beings are simply "bundles of electromagnetic energy" in what looks like an ordinary human body. We are constantly expressing that energy in the ways we think about things and in the countless emotions that course through our systems, and more often than not, we're quite undisciplined about the whole process. Alas, there is no class or program, to my knowledge, that trains us in the art of being "Disciplined Humans" from birth onward into adolescence and then adulthood.

I do my best to look at this Life as an extraordinary gift, an opportunity to express the Divine Being-ness, GOD. However, you want to refer to that source of Life energy pulsating through me and you and out into the World. When I remember that I've got 86,400 seconds in my day today and that they're mine to use any way I choose, it ups the ante for me considerably. I also know there are no mistakes and that I have always been in the right place at the right time. Did I always know that or believe that? Of course not! I spent too many years blaming others for my various Life situations, always internally debating how or why someone else was slimmer or better looking. Since carrying extra weight has been an issue for me most of my Life, I've wasted a great deal of time feeling bad about myself and for judging everyone else on my own "feeling less than" internal scale. I have also spent considerable time and energy apologizing and energetically erasing those "oh so bad, so sad" unproductive and non-Life-giving thoughts. How silly of me to wish or even imagine ill will to someone for being skinnier than I or more good looking? But that too is human nature, and I am quite human. Do you have any issues like this in your own Life that trip you up? Probably so, and if you do we can work on that together. I'd like to think that unproductive phase is behind me, and one can only hope, but at least I've learned how to catch it sooner and attempt to "erase" the damage before it leaks out too far into the World.

My first dedicated Metaphysical teacher, Thomas R. Sandell, later Shri Bodhisattva, was always "erasing the air" with large sweeps of his hand as he would laugh and shake his head in dismay. With his deep, booming voice he would say, "I let another thought escape, and I had to catch it before it did too much damage!" I am eternally grateful that I had him as a teacher; he was flawed, human, and brilliant, and he trusted me with his knowledge. With each subsequent client, I've tried to honor him and the trust he placed in me with his teaching and his grasp of the Universe at large.

From his 1987 book, *XIO The Philosophy of Energy*, quintessential Renaissance Man and tireless researcher, Millard Deutsch says: "All the great masters, mystics, saints, and sages had a great knowledge of Energy. Or in STAR WARS jargon, great knowledge of the "Ways of the Force." In fact you might say that knowledge of Energy is truly the graduate course into the higher planes."

*Miracles do not happen in contradiction to Nature, but only in contradiction to that which is known to us in Nature.*
~ St. Augustine

As the Buddhist sages tell us, there is a spark of each of us in one another and a spark of GOD in everything that has ever been created. The greeting, "***Namaste***," means just that:

"When I am in that place within myself where I truly know who I am, and you are in that place as well, then there can only be one of us."

Coming from the Indian Sanskrit, Namaste has many translations and can be used to greet one another or to part ways. Essentially, it comes from *namah* which means to bow in adoration, and the pronoun *te* which means to you. So no matter what the rest of the explanation might be, you are "bowing in adoration to the one in front of you."

What a lovely World this could be if we approached anyone and everyone in front of us with that type of adoration. No need for titles, any background check, employment status, or pedigree. Simply acknowledging the God Force Being in front of us is quite enough.

My study of Buddhism and various other traditions have taught me to radically expand my concept of GOD or the Divine Being-ness from that of a lovely man with warm eyes, long flowing hair, and his hands outstretched. Even as I continue my internal work at being more inclusive, I must admit this Irish Catholic girl from

Buffalo finds that to be oddly comforting and appealing. But I also understand that image to be only a concept and that we owe it to ourselves to keep exploring, be more curious, and to stretch our imaginations. As I mentioned at the opening of this book, our family of origin religious beliefs that we heard over and over again in the home and at church are strong points of reference for sure. But I think we owe it to ourselves to become curious and dedicated explorers in our own right. Those religious beliefs will still be there waiting for you at the end of this chapter. I promise you that.

Consider this for a moment. As each thought that you have emerges, it takes on its own momentum as it begins its swirling, tumbling, circling movement out into the Universe. Once that thought leaves you ~ and it happens in an instant ~ it has a Life of its own and is very hard to grab back and or change.

My hope with this book is to encourage you to be open to developing new sensitivities and to think of the World in much larger terms than ever before. Rather than just moving through your days in a hum-drum way, I want to encourage you to keep growing your consciousness. Remember when you were five or eight years of age and every day was full of one new adventure after another? Pretend that you are that again, unafraid of the journey and delightfully curious.

When our curiosity is piqued, we can tap into the magic of all that surrounds us with much less resistance. From work I've done in the past with noted Metaphysical teacher, Stuart Wilde, and from my friend and colleague, Anke Nowicki of Light Partners, I've learned to look at the World with different eyes and to hear with a new set of ears. In the World that was Stuart Wilde's domain, he was always encouraging students to raise their vibration to such a higher level as to be impervious to any harm from outside sources. From Anke Nowicki, Homeopathic Healer and Radionics Practitioner, I have learned the dramatic difference between "the Social Mind construct" that guides most of the population and elevating oneself to that realm of conscious behavior governed by Divine forces of light and love. If you are operating under the guidance and direction of God/The Divine Source, don't you think your Life might be operating at a higher frequency?

Sound different to you? They're not, just slightly different jargon meant to encourage us to strive for a better reality and remove ourselves from the lower consciousness realms of intention ~ thought ~ and, ultimately, action.

In recent years, our knowledge about Quantum Physics (QP) and Quantum Mechanics (QM) has grown exponentially, allowing us to broaden our perception of what's possible. Just as personal coaches can help a struggling athlete or performer to internally visualize their success on the playing field or the stage, so can we visualize healing of our own bodies or commanding the functioning of our own body/mind/brain system.

We in the Western World can get easily tripped up by various Religious theories that were intentionally designed to keep us trapped in limited thinking. Learn to talk back to those bad thinking patterns when they pop up ~ instead, claim your power by stating out loud:

"No!! I don't think that way any longer! I am a magical, miraculous and mystical being in a physical body and I am capable of creating the best Life possible!"

"I am meant to be a creative thinker, charting my own course in Life, without the baggage of original sin or any threats of a hellish afterlife!"

Think about yourself as a brilliant network of energetic potential, an entity that can be trained and directed in any number of ways. Perhaps you've already had an experience where you felt in your gut that you had to change something immediately, and you did. Maybe you avoided a car accident, or slicing your finger off while chopping vegetables, or not dropping a heavy piece of equipment on your foot. In each instance you had a simultaneous "vision" of what could go wrong, while also having an equally empowering "vision" of how to avoid the damage. Your internal network of electromagnetic energy shot into motion so quickly there was no perceptible pattern of thought to action. That's just an example of how fast it all happens. As we become increasingly more aware of this action, and then teach ourselves how to make the best use of this automatic skill set, we become more deliberate human beings on every level.

Quantum Mechanics has questioned the material foundations of the World by demonstrating in the laboratory that atoms and subatomic particles are not solid objects. We now also know from the study of Quantum Physics that whatever is being observed and the observer are linked. As observer's conclusion changes, so does what is being observed change. These concepts have been widely accepted for a number of years, initially through the works of scientific wizards like Max Planck,

Niels Bohr, and Albert Einstein. Rather than researching those early 1900's scientific papers, you can check out more recent publications in more up to date language. For instance, "The Biology of Belief" by stem-cell biologist, Bruce Lipton, "Deep Truth" by New York Times best-selling author of "The Divine Matrix" and "Fractal Time," Gregg Braden, and most recently, "Breaking The Habit of Being Yourself" by functional brain expert and the author of "Evolve Your Brain," Dr. Joe Dispenza.

*Every great and deep difficulty bears in itself its own solution.*
*It forces us to change our thinking in order to find it.*
~ Niels Bohr, Nobel Prize-Winning Physicist

In the next chapter, I'll go into more detail about how to direct specific information as a means of helping your Life move forward with greater ease and clarity of purpose. To my way of thinking, the more tools we have at our disposal, the more exciting our lives become on our own personal journeys toward self-discovery and self-mastery.

I have learned so much from my study of the Unity Principles and through the study of the Science of Mind philosophy set forth by Dr. Ernest Holmes. Both of these esteemed teachings stress the importance of personal responsibility and the birthright we all share as deserving Children of God. Founded in 1889 in Kansas City, Missouri, by Charles and Myrtle Fillmore, Unity's Mission Statement is "To help and serve through prayer, publishing, and community." According to Unity, "God is the one power, all good, everywhere present, all wisdom." In my version of that, God is in all things, everywhere all at once, all the time, or there is no place that God is not.

"The Science of Mind" originally published in 1926 and then later revised in 1938 by Dr. Ernest Holmes provides us with a simple explanation of why our thoughts have power and how we can change our Life by changing our thinking. From "How To Change Your Life" by Holmes, "Everything that exists is a manifestation of the Divine Mind; but the Divine Mind, being inexhaustible and limitless, is never caught in any form; it is merely expressed by that form."

As I stated at the beginning of this chapter, everything in Life involves the movement of energy, every thought and every emotion we experience. My former teacher, Shri Brahmananda Sarasvati taught me that behind my physical and physiological body, there is a body of electricity. As we learn to investigate, communicate with, and ultimately move in harmony with these electrical impulses, or the movement of energy, we become better operators of our own body/mind/spirit instrument. That to me is a journey worth taking. I'm hoping it is for you as well.

*What is the difference between deep sleep and meditation? In deep sleep, psychological or psychosomatic consciousness, the body, and the mind ~ all three are sleeping. But during dynamic meditation, the individual I AM or the psychological consciousness is transformed into the universal I AM, while the body and mind remain in deep sleep.*
~ Shri Brahmananda Sarasvati 1986

## Action Steps

Using the journal pages provided here or working in your own journal, make some observations you've had while reading this chapter. Sit quietly and ask yourself these questions:

Am I now more open to cultures other than my own?

Did anything here especially pique my imagination?

# Chapter Nine

## Healing Modalities and the Chakra System

In each system of healing that I have studied, the concept that we are one with all of humanity and all of nature has been understood as accepted beliefs. Also, in each of these various practices, the concept of personal Self-awareness has been a driving force for not only individual good, but for the good of the whole as well. That means you and me and the whole of humanity, everything in the World.

In the study of the *Touch for Health System,* created by John F. Thie, D.C., in the early 1970s, I was introduced to the concept of kinesiology (from the Ancient Greek word kinesis meaning movement) when I studied this system in the 1980s. As a practical guide to natural health, using acupressure in combination with massage and a renewed overall awareness of the body as a whole, we can embrace the connectedness of all of our parts to one another. Dr. Thie also introduced an updated version of the actual "body clock," which affects each organ of the body and every body system as well. This is one of the reasons why I've never advocated for Daylight Saving Time, as it throws our internal clocks "off" When it's in effect, I always keep a clock set to Standard Time on the hutch in my dining room so I can glance at it daily to help stabilize my internal organs and internal body clock. Try it yourself and see if you notice even the most subtle of internal changes. It might also help you to get a better night's sleep.

Although there are countless systems and practices with which to monitor the constant movement of energy through the body, it's important to consider the Meridian System and the Chakra System before branching out into other studies.

The Meridian System is a complex, intricate system which follows the continuous flow of energy from one part of the body to another.

As the diagram below shows, there is one continuous flow of energetic movement throughout the entire physical body. This energetic flow allows our Life Force

Energy to remain balanced, healthy, and functional, with each system communicating flawlessly with the next.

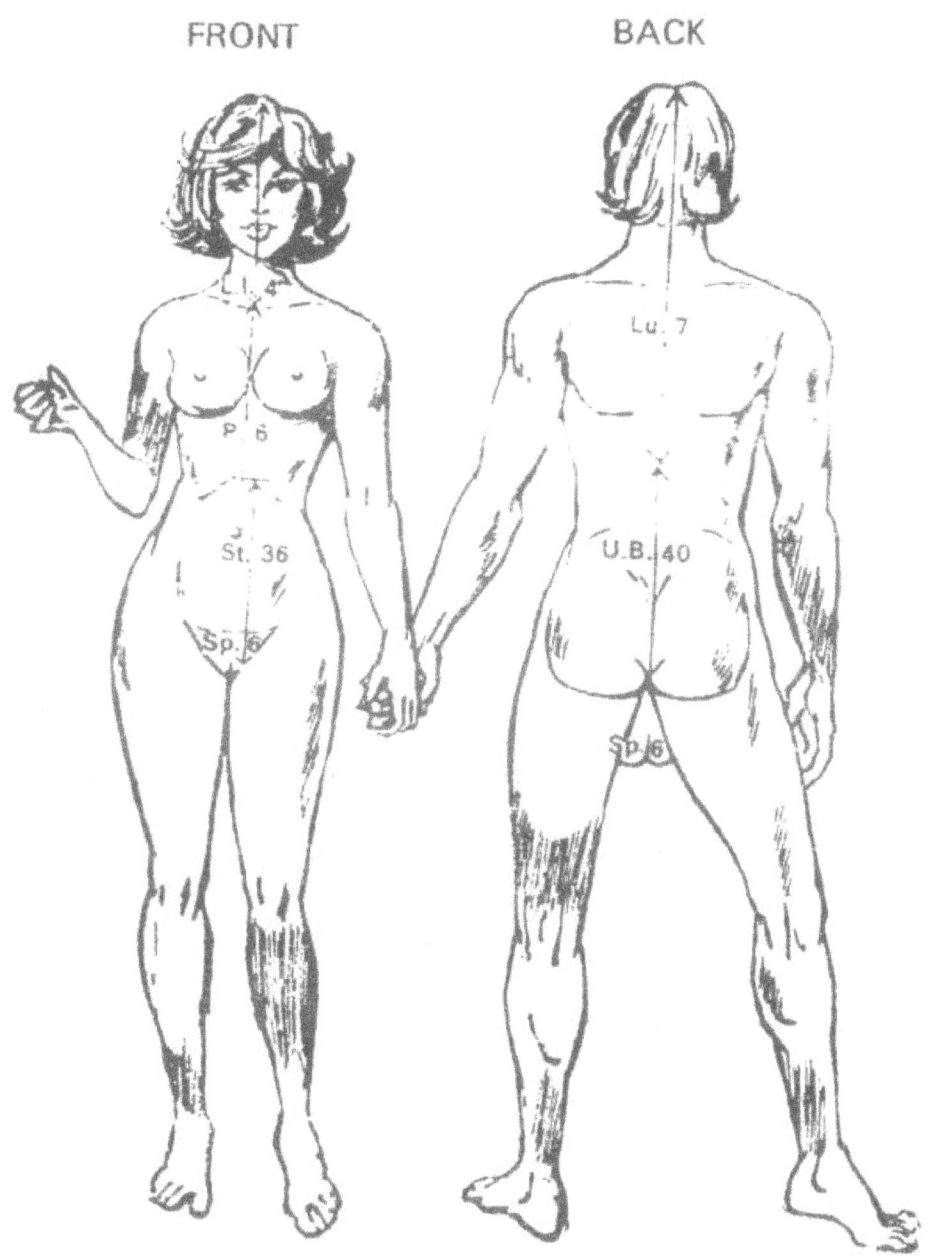

"Central and Governing Vessel"

This diagram is from a book of acupuncture healing from Laos, but the image is quite common in the World of chiropractic and EFT and all Oriental healing practices.

As the *Touch for Health* manuscript explains, these meridian lines provide a massive framework for the body's innate energetic intelligence to operate within.

The Central Meridian, sometimes referred to as "The Conception Vessel" is YIN or female in nature and runs up the front of the body. Originating from the center of the pubic bone, the Central Meridian runs up the center of the body, under the chin to just below the lower lip. Supporting many of the body and energy functions, The Central Meridian calms the body, the heart, and the mind and is also associated with the functions of the nervous system and the brain.

The Governing Meridian, which is YANG or masculine in nature, runs up the center of your body from the coccyx/tailbone, up the entire length of the spine, over the top of your head and down the face to the center of the upper lip. We don't think of the skin as being an actual organ of the body, but it most certainly is, and it serves as one of our first lines of defense against illness and internal disruptions. The Governing Meridian is the Meridian associated with the skin.

Although Meridians are not anatomical structures, and scientists have not found any evidence of their existence, to any student of Chiropractic work or any of the many Oriental practices, they are most certainly real, operating constantly for our betterment and ease of body function and health.

*The Conception and Governing vessels are like midnight and midday. They are the polar axis of the body – there is one source and the two branches. One goes to the front and the other to the back of the body. When we try to divide these, we see that yin and yang are inseparable. When we try to see them as one, we see that is an indivisible whole.*
~ Li Shi-Zhen, sixteenth century Chinese Acupuncturist and Herbalist

Among the practices that commonly accept and rely on the movement of energy through the Meridian system are Chiropractic care, *Touch for Health*, Hypnotherapy, Thought Field Therapy, EFT or Emotional Freedom Technique, commonly known as Tapping, Jin Shin Jyutsu, The Kabbalah, The Huna System of Natural Healing, Usui Shiki Ryoho Reiki Healing and others I have not personally studied. Even when I am in the midst of a Hypnotherapy session with someone, I always reference the movement of the breath as it flows through the whole-body system.

### The Wheel from *Touch for Health*

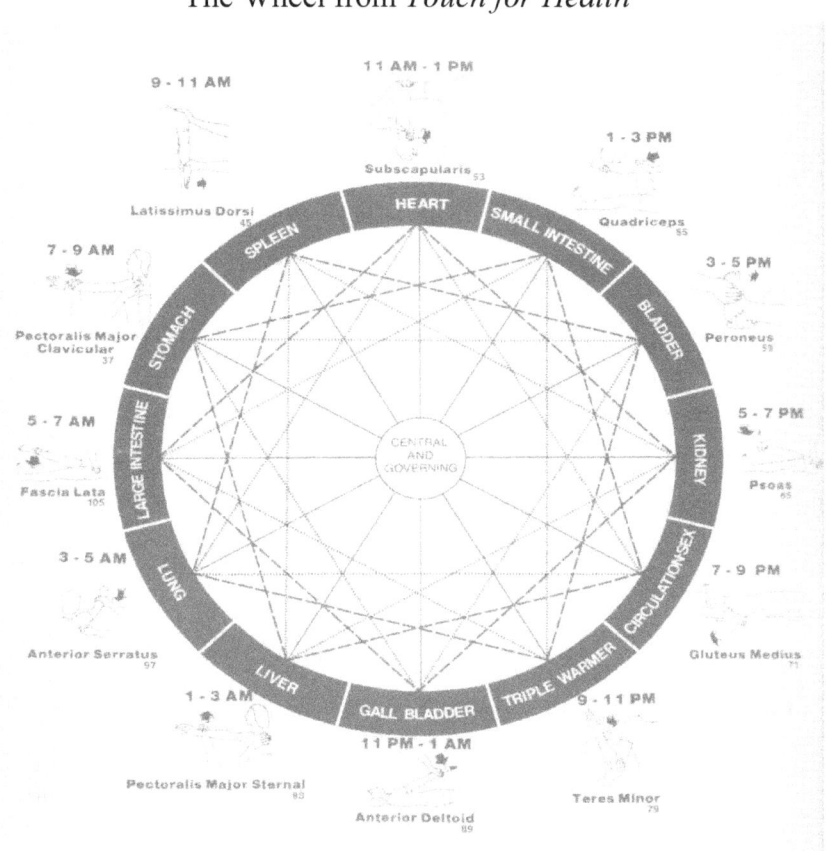

"The Wheel" from *Touch for Health*

Source: *Touch for Health* by John F. Thie and D.C., written in 1973 and revised in 1979. Published by DeVorss & Company, 1046 Princeton Drive, Marina del Rey, California, 902291

*Sooner or later, we come to the edge of a vastness that has been there all along and we are forced to decide if we are visitors or if this is our home.*
~ Mark Nepo

Before I move on to the Chakra System, I want to touch on the Theory of The Five Elements. Known not only in The *Touch for Health* System but to all Indigenous tribes and throughout the studies of Oriental Medicine. The Five Elements are not chemical Elements but rather five aspects of the World. These are the five essences which represent the cycles of the Earth.

According to "The Tao of Health" by Michael Blate:

> "In the Birth phase of the Universe arose *wood* – all growing matter.
> In its surging upward phase, *Fire* – air, gases.
> In its mature adult phase, *Earth* – dirt, soil.
> In its decay phase, *metal* – all inorganic matter.
> In its death/rebirth phase, *Water* – all moisture."

The diagram from the *Touch for Health* book illustrates that every segment of the body is connected by energy lines, which create a Fire- pointed star pattern. According to Dr. John F. Thie, D.C., "The wheel below represents the flow of the meridian energy, each meridian being represented by a section of the wheel rim. By moving around the wheel in a clockwise direction, we can follow the flow of energy through the entire 12-meredian system. The lines within the wheel denote subsidiary energy flows.

In each system I've studied, the five Elements mentioned are all represented. Although they may hold different positions and reference points, they are all considered necessary to our well-being and overall state of healthful awareness. As humans, we naturally are made up of each natural element. It is also worth noting that the mystical Star of David, generally accepted as a symbol of Jewish identity and Judaism, is actually a symbol which has been known for centuries as a means of bringing Spirit into Matter. As a deviation from the Seal of Solomon, this hexagram shape is composed of two equilateral triangles, which holds great esoteric meaning. It is believed to be a key to the evolution of Humanity.

The Seal of Solomon was used not only for decorative purposes but also as a deep mystical symbolism by Muslims and Kabbalistic Jews alike. It has been estimated that the Jewish people of Prague adopted the symbol in the seventeenth century.

In the study of the 6-Heart Virtues, which is worth investigating, this Star of David pattern is once again used as the central focus to illustrate both the color spectrum and the aspects of an open, virtuous heart.

The more I study, the more there is to learn and to grow into, making me more eager than ever to embrace unique and compelling topics of study to keep my mind sharp and my body in the best state of health possible at every juncture of my incredible LIFE!

I never want to miss one moment of this extraordinary gift from the Divine Creator, and I'm sure you don't want anything less than the best level of health possible.

## Specific Healing Modalities

**Hypnotherapy** ~ Although I have studied many different versions of hypnotherapy, I am most comfortable with Ericksonian Hypnosis. You can find a qualified teacher or learn more by referencing the Milton H. Erickson Foundation online. Of the many systems I've worked with, this made the most sense to me and I feel most at home when working with clients in this modality. Naturally, my comfort level is transmitted to anyone I am working with, which also helps me to connect on an even deeper level.

**Emotional Freedom Technique (EFT)** ~ My first introduction to this was through the work of Gary Craig, the Founder of what is now called "Optimal EFT/The Unseen Therapist." If you feel so led, you can contact Gary at garycraig@emofree.com. There are a number of helpful EFT scripts and videos on his website, so please check them out. I always appreciate knowing another practitioner's approach and what works or doesn't work for them. My original EFT teacher was the wise and beloved Bea Scarlata, M.A., L.P.C., who embraced me from the get-go with love and compassion. Her all-encompassing acceptance of my childhood trauma and her solid belief in my ability to heal were, in themselves, Life changing and inspirational. We all need to be seen, heard, and accepted.

I have also enjoyed working with Nick Ortner from The Tapping Solution. If his name sparks recognition in you, please follow through and reach out to Nick at thetappingsolution.com. He is also the author of a book by the same name, published in 2013 and containing a number of excellent EFT scripts to help you understand and practice with the techniques for yourself.

If you're like me, presentation and the resonance of a person's voice can make all the difference in whether I make a good connection or not. This is especially important in hypnosis, tapping, or any hands-on healing techniques, so get online and listen to both of these men before committing to either technique.

**Jin Shin Jyutsu** ~ Commonly translated to mean "Getting to KNOW/HELP MYSELF.' For centuries, ancient peoples used JSJ to heal themselves and others. It was rediscovered in the early twentieth century by Master Jiro Murai, a Japanese healer and philosopher who first sought this out to heal himself. One of his most dedicated students, Mary Burmeister, introduced JSJ to the Western World in the early 1960s. Now taught Worldwide, this practice of massaging specific pressure points involves the whole-body system in the overall healing process. To find a qualified teacher in your area, simply get online and search for "Jin Shin Jyutsu" and proceed from there. This is a technique I use every day working with all of the actual placements on the fingers and the palm of the hand. This technique is now commonly found in not only hospital settings, but in many therapeutic practices. My first introduction to Jin Shin Jyutsu came through noted practitioner, Jennifer

Bradley from Lexington, KY, who is a unique and focused healing resource for many.

Confident not only in her own abilities, but Jennifer is also a mighty advocate for anyone fortunate enough to be on the receiving end of her power and absolute resolve to manifest the best possible outcome.

**The Kabbalah** ~ I was first introduced to the Kabbalah while studying at the Aquarian Research Center in WPB, FLA and I became mesmerized by its depth and secrecy. The Kabbalah is essentially the ancient mystical interpretation of the Jewish Bible, arising first as an oral tradition. My teacher taught that the Kabbalah was only "transmitted" from one Kabbalistic Jewish Rabbi to his eldest son, who had attained the age of 40 and was in an ongoing, committed sexual relationship. Such was considered to be the power one was afforded by unlocking the secrets of the Tree of Life. Kabbalah translates to "reception, tradition" and I believe it is a sacred study to be approached with reverence and a sense of deep appreciation. If I were to look for a qualified teacher today, I would first approach local Synagogues to inquire if the teaching is available now to the local community. As with all such important steps, you must inquire within yourself first and then trust the answers you get beyond ego or simple curiosity.

**The Huna System of Natural Healing** ~ Huna is a practical system of psychology long used by the *Kahuna* of ancient Hawaii. For centuries, these wise teachers guarded their powerful secret. Huna, the Hawaiian word for *secret*, was the name given by Max Freedom Long, the courageous and open-minded scholar who brought this psycho-religious healing method into the World. The *Kahunas*, or *keepers of the secret*, were adept at healing the sick, untangling financial issues and social difficulties and solving personal problems as they "changed the future" for the better. When working with a Huna practitioner, the person must first permit the work, then acknowledge that there is a Higher Source assisting, and that the Huna practitioner is simply a channel or a conduit for the healing energies to enliven the recipient's own natural Life-force energies. I was first introduced to Huna by my beloved teacher, Thomas R. Sandell (later Shri Bodhisattva), and it was a Life changer. If this sparks any internal interest for you, then touch base with Huna Research, Inc. in Cape Girardeau, Missouri, for classes and perhaps even a teacher in your area, or you may search out Max Freedom Long for detailed current information.

**Usui Shiki Ryoho Traditional Reiki Healing** ~ Reiki, pronounced "ray- key" is a Japanese word meaning Universal Life Force Energy. It is this energy which emanates from the hands of a Reiki Therapist. The Reiki system of healing is Zen Buddhist in origin and is over 2500 years old. Since it is universal energy, anyone may use it and benefit from its use, regardless of their particular creed, religion, or background. Usui Shiki Ryoho means, "The Usui System of Natural Healing," named after Dr. Mikao Usui, President of the Doshisha University, a Christian school in Kyoto, Japan. His relentless search to unlock the keys to Reiki have given the World a tool to create lasting physical healing, along with mental and emotional health as well.

Taught in 3 distinct levels, Reiki is now commonly accepted as a usable, noninvasive, and accurate healing method in use by nurses and other health practitioners in not only hospitals, but also in nursing homes and rehabilitation facilities. I was greatly privileged to have studied with the first occidental (non-Oriental) Reiki Master, Virginia W. Samdahl, a woman of high principles and a consummate master level teacher.

Try reaching out to your local Health Food Store, Metaphysical shop, or simply do an online search for qualified "traditional" Reiki practitioners in your area if you're interested in pursuing this further. I use Reiki daily in my personal Life and with every client I am privileged enough to work with. The 2nd Level Reiki training includes the projection of symbols from me to anyone sitting in front of me or via FaceTime or Zoom. I assume, in each case, that I have permission to use the symbols, along with anything else in my considerable "toolbox," since you've made the appointment to work with me. Don't you agree?

# The Chakra System

The Chakras were first mentioned in the Vedas, ancient sacred texts of spiritual knowledge dating from 1500 to 1000 BC. The word *Chakra* translates to a "disc" or a "wheel" and refers to specific energy points within the physical body. When I began studying at the Aquarian Research Center in WPB, FLA, I was taught there are seven major Chakras and 114 minor Chakras, which affect every area of our bodily functions and hence, our lives. Over the years, I understand that various systems offer any number of variations, but the common theme of spinning vortexes of energy remains a constant. In many systems, it is an accepted belief that there are 21 Minor Chakras, so take your pick. These Seven Major Chakras run from the base of your spine to the top of your head, and they are always in motion.

If something is "off kilter" in one Chakra, the energy cannot travel in an appropriate smooth, healthy line, interrupting the flow of energy from one Chakra to another and potentially resulting in anything from irritability to actual physical illness. If the interruption is severe enough, and not balanced properly, and subsequently allowed to go untreated, death will occur.

In one class I attended, taught by an esteemed Hindu teacher from India, he encouraged us to remember the colors associated with the Chakras with this silly little rhyme:

"Real Old Yokels, Gorge Beef In Volume"

The Chakras are always referred to from the bottom (Root) to the top (Crown), beginning with red at the Root Chakra. As the diagram below illustrates, these are meant to be moving centers of energy in perpetual motion.

As you can see from the diagram, The Chakra System is an intricate, always in motion, connected network of energetic fields. The location of the seven major chakras on the physical body corresponds to the major nerve centers/bundles governing actual physical organs. For instance, the Root/Base Charka *Muladhara* (red) corresponds to the adrenals, kidneys, and the spine. The 2nd Sacral/Chakra *Svadhisthana* (orange) corresponds to the reproductive system, including the ovaries and the prostate. The 3rd Solar Plexus/Chakra, *Manipura*, (yellow) corresponds to the pancreas, liver, gallbladder, and the gastrointestinal system. The 4th Heart/Chakra *Anahata* (green) corresponds to the magnetized field of the heart. The 5th Throat/Chakra *Vishuddha* (blue) represents our truth, both spoken and silent. The 6th Brow/Chakra, Ajna, (indigo) is involved with our creative and intuitive functioning. And finally our 7th Crown/Chakra *Sahasrara* (violet) corresponds to our witness self, our spiritual link or connection to ourselves, others, and that which is most highly connected and receptive to the Divine.

The Sacred Symbology associated with each Chakra is a study in and of itself, but if you choose to delve into this further, you will see commonalities of shape and design from one system to another. Perhaps it would be wise to begin your Chakra journey with a qualified Yoga Instructor or even a Traditionally trained Usui Shiki Ryoho Reiki Practitioner.

Having studied for years with Bio-energetic Researcher, Homeopath and Radionics Practitioner Anke Nowicki from Light Partners, I have been beyond Blessed to learn how to look at the body with a refreshed set of eyes. Specializing in the combined use of homeopathic light and color application and sacred psychology traditions as a modality for expanding consciousness, Anke is one of the most well-trained practitioners I've ever encountered. It helps that she is endlessly inquisitive and quite brilliant! Having trained in the field of Radionics with the work of British researchers, Dr. David Tansley and Keith Mason, Anke's methods of specific color applications to remove emotional blockages at the cellular and energetic levels only deepened. You can search her out online at "Anke Nowicki and Light Partners." If her name resonates with you, please reach out to her at once, as her schedule remains booked with serious clients and students of Life.

In his book, *Radionics and the Subtle Bodies of Man*, Dr. David Tansley states "the Seven Major Chakras are formed at the points where the standing lines of light cross over each other 21 times." Another excellent source of information is *Hands of Light: A Guide to Healing Through the Human Energy Field* by Barbara Ann Brennan. Written in 1987, this book paved the way for a deeper understanding of who we are as human beings, in all of our intricate facets and mystical layers. I bought the book in March of 1988 while still a student at The Aquarian Research Center in WPB, FLA and I am still in awe of its detailed diagrams and insightful research. Before I buy any book, I always look to see who it is dedicated to and what the opening quotes might be. In this case, "This book is dedicated to all travelers on the path homeward," and the first quote is from one of my all-time favorites.

*I maintain that cosmic religious feeling is the strongest and noblest incitement to scientific research.* ~ Albert Einstein

I find that a thorough understanding of the Chakra System to be the basis of every healing modality, including so many ancient cultural and mystical overlays; it's simply awe inspiring to me. I could talk about it for another 20 pages and never cover it all. Perhaps, for yourself, by embracing this concept, researching it as it pertains to your own Life and any on-going or past health issues, your sense of self and your entire World will be richly enhanced and all the better for it.

Here's to our healthy, sparkling, spinning vortexes of Divine Light, ever balanced and full of good health, power, and wisdom.

## Action Steps

Using the journal pages provided here or working in your own journal, sit quietly for a few moments as you gather your thoughts about this last chapter.

What experiences have you had with alternative Healing Modalities?

If you have not been exposed to these practices, are you now more willing to explore your alternative options?

After reading the information on the Chakra System, are you now more curious about delving deeper into this system?

# Chapter Ten

## Psychic Self Defense

It might be an odd concept that we should prepare for or even consider the topic of *Psychic Self-Defense,* but my years of training have taught me otherwise. As people just going about our day-to-day lives, we tend to be careless with our thoughts. Actually, we are quite reckless as we tend to *carelessly sling* many less-than-ideal opinions, attitudes and our own brands of *shoulds* out there to land on whatever and on whomever is closest to that rocket of muck.

Because I know I am a well-trained Metaphysician, I have the following list available to glance at daily:

What do you think?
How can I know if it's true?
Where did that thought come from?
Who is in charge of my thought process?
What path is that thought going to take?
What is the purpose of that thought?
Who might it harm?
Is it necessary?
How can I monitor and possibly alter or stop the process?

I also have another sign which reads: **N.O.M.B.**, which is short for, None Of My Business!

If it's not about me, I do not need to engage or have an opinion or any internal conversation. Wow, that's hard, and it's something I must remain aware of at all times. As a Libra with a Libra Rising and a Capricorn Moon, my brain moves fast. It is quite opinionated. If I don't maintain a steady level of discipline, I am in a jam that does not lead to happy consequences. If someone is paying me for answers, that's another story and I have permission to address a multitude of issues.

*Just as an aside, there are only three types of business: my business, your business and God's business, and if I am minding anyone else's business but my own, I am out of line.*

And that goes for you, too!! **N. O. M. B.**

Our mind/brain systems are brilliant instruments, but only when we have done adequate training to learn how to manage them can we operate them with some level of maturity. Self-awareness is the key, and that's so much of what this whole book is about. I always hold out hope for all of humanity as a species, but we all know there are people in the World who are **not happy**, and if they're not happy, no one else should be either. You've met them too, the grumps, the complainers, the bigots, the cruel racists, *the just plain old mean and nasty ones*. Even as I work at sending these folks as much genuine love and light as possible, I still don't want their **rockets of muck** to land back on me. And I am assuming you'd rather not be a target, either. When I say, "I send them love and light" that means I am not actively engaging with them, nor am I making up mean and nasty stories about them either. Cruelty invites cruelty, and I endeavor to maintain a neutral position, projecting equilibrium as best I can. My classic internal statement is, "God Bless You!"

I've covered some of this in various parts of this book but I am going to give you *my current daily routine* before I ever leave the house. Do not become overwhelmed. Like any habit, it takes a little bit of practice to claim it as your own, and I'd very much like you to claim some or part of this for yourself. Tailor it to your Life and needs, but only after you have mastered the basics.

## Rosemary's Usual Protection Routine

Before leaving the house I open a MAP Coning for myself by asking to be connected with the Over-Lighting Deva of Healing with great love and respect. I ask that I be kept healthy, safe, and protected from all harm and that I remember to be a good, kind human being to all who cross my path. I then ask to be connected with PAN, the Guardian of The Earth Realm, asking for health and safety in all of my encounters and I ask this Nature Spirit to be as big and bold as possible for my safety and protection. Between calling on these timeless, and gracious entities, I always pause for about ten seconds as I wait to feel their energies descending upon me and wrapping me up. Next I call upon my own personal White Brotherhood Medical Unit/The Illumined Ones, asking for good health, protection, safety and guidance to go about my day with the most balanced sense of myself possible. I also ask these sometimes enormous, shape-shifting beings to be as big, bold and colorful as they choose to be. Finally, I ask that that aspect of my own Higher Self/Consciousness taking part in the MAP Coning to be alert to my good, taking part in that days safety, protection and guidance, keeping me aware, healthy and protected at all times.

*** I think it's important to note here that we as human beings are not alone, that we belong to a Universal Collective that includes all of the Nature Spirits, Devas, Angels, and every living creature on the Planet. Putting our natural arrogance aside is an important step in our healing and our long-term well-being as servants to a greater good. ***

As I pull out of my driveway, I also state out loud the words to the Lord Michael Blessing, as I vividly imagine a clear white light surrounding my vehicle, myself, and anything that might touch my Life that day:

> *Lord Michael to the front,*
> *Lord Michael to the rear,*
> *Lord Michael to the right,*
> *Lord Michael to the left,*
> *Lord Michael above,*
> *Lord Michael below,*
> *Lord Michael, Lord Michael wherever I go!*

If I am going to a medical or dental appointment and am the least bit uneasy about it, or if I'm overly tired or stressed, I also ask that Lord Michael the Arch Angel stand in front of me, that Arch Angel Raphael stands at my right, Arch Angel Uriel is at my back and Arch Angel Gabriel is at my left side, all with their backs to me, facing outward to intercept any potential issue or harm. I also ask for my own personal Guardian Angel, **Betty,** to be in charge of everything. That includes me, the Arch Angels, the MAP team ~ you name it, and **Betty** is the overarching presence keeping us all in line. I can hear her laughing at me now. She does that quite often. At first it offended me, but now I am not the least put off by it, and I just laugh at myself with her.

Depending on the circumstances, I may also ask to be wrapped up in several layers of tumbled black tourmaline encrusted Saran Wrap. I imagine myself wrapped up from head to toe with openings for my eyes, nose, mouth and ears. I also use Thieves Oil on the roof of my mouth and across the upper and lower gum lines to protect me from any airborne bacterial, fungal or viral infections. You can buy Thieves Oil from any Young Living Oil distributor or perhaps from your Chiropractor or healthcare practitioner. I also carry a spray bottle in my purse to refresh the protection if I think it's necessary.

I then unravel all of these things during my nighttime shower, being sure to thank everyone involved for keeping me safe, aware, healthy and peaceful throughout the day. Showering off the day is a must for me to keep myself healthy and balanced, allowing any **muck** to wash down the drain. If you're a morning shower person, you might consider switching to before bed for a month just to see if you feel fresher and more relaxed.

I just heard you luxurious bathers groan ~ you can do that too at night, but you must end it with a **shower to wash off the day** completely.

I always carry my own water with me, usually with a fresh slice of lemon for good measure. With the best of intentions, I also try to leave the house in a timely manner since I know that rushing is never good for our nervous system. I tend to fail at this routinely, yet I remain hopeful. It's vital to remember that our natural state of being is to be healthy and to be safe. However, the busier the world gets, the busier we seem to get, which inadvertently thwarts our usual equilibrium. Think about this scenario: you're feeling fine, looking good, and all set for a day or an evening of productivity and wonderful fun. Then you walk into a home or a building, or a person suddenly passes by at close range, and you're crestfallen, totally deflated. It's as if the darkness has descended, and you feel out of place, awkward, and totally ill at ease. Perhaps you're even sick to your stomach and or momentarily dizzy. Maybe you even develop an acute case of diarrhea.

The grumpies have arrived, accompanied by the perpetually out of sorts complainers, bigots, racists, or just the plain old mean and nasty ones. And they have dumped their **buckets of muck** all over you. But here's the thing: if that's their usual state of being, and my guess is that it probably is, then they have no idea what happened. Those grumpies are so accustomed to their dismal state of being that they have nothing else as a reference point. It may be hard to fathom, but some people are unaccustomed to living in a state of joy, preferring to remain in their usual state of "**woe is me**/ain't it awful/it'll never work/I can never catch a break/It's all **their** fault" routine of Life. Bless them! Decide to never join their club, the membership is already way too full.

**If you ever find yourself in this scenario**, get up and move around. As you do so, inhale as deeply as possible through the nose and blow out the offending energy with gusto through your mouth. Then if possible, go outside and breathe in the freshness of the outdoors, as you inhale through the nose and exhale strongly through your mouth. If you can find a sunny spot to stand in, go there since the rays of the Sun are cleansing and naturally balancing. Clap your hands together a couple of times and shake out those hands as you quite literally shake off the disturbance. It is also wise in situations like this to ask yourself: "Is this mine?" ~ chances are you'll hear a definite NO, alerting you to the fact that you've just been impressed with the sadness/pain/illness/fear or whatever of another person. Then do your best to avoid contact with the **bringers of the muck**. If you must remain in their presence, wrap them in as many layers of pink cotton candy as necessary to render them harmless. That way, whatever they are trying to send out to you sticks to them instead. Be resolute in your desire to not engage with them on any level ~ even creating an opinion about them is a level of engagement. Don't go there!

**Your breath** is always your first and foremost line of defense. In a tense or frightening situation, the more you breathe, the better the outcome. If you inadvertently hold your breath, you are literally "swallowing the pain or the panic/fear" rather than releasing it.

EXERCISE: Take a full, deep breath in through the nose, and then immediately expel the breath with force and determination through your mouth as you imagine that you have just blown out the problem, the person, or the situation. The more you work with your breath, and as you make friends with your breath as if you've just met for the first time, make it your intention to find your own personal CENTER through the breath and then decide to live there fearlessly and comfortably.

**To disconnect** from an unpleasant person or situation, simply do the following:

EXERCISE: As always, begin by working with your breathing, then immediately turn your back on the source of the negative input, brush off your entire Solar Plexus (that whole area in the front center of your body from below the bustline to the lower abdomen), using your hands like a feather duster moving from top to bottom and tossing the energy away from your body. Do not respond to the source of the negativity in any way, don't dwell on the encounter or the conversation, being mindful not to be mulling it over in your mind, trying to make course corrections. It's done. Move on. And by all means, resist the urge to retell the story to anyone else as you'll only conjure up the entire incident again, giving it even more oomph and power than before.

**To end an argument**, stop participating in it! Thoughts and actions follow energy. If someone is yelling at you, it's time for you to get very quiet and still.

EXERCISE: Being mindful, as always, of your breathing, drop your voice, change your body language, and allow your anger to flow through you rather than trying to stop it or to stuff it. If the confrontation is still in progress, start using different language, "I understand your fear, pain, anger, etc." "I realize you're mad" "I am hearing what you are saying" As you maintain your equilibrium, with a lowered voice and a calm demeanor, being mindful of using deliberate body blocking language, chances are the situation will de-escalate quickly. Body blocking language looks like crossing your arms across your entire chest with one hand resting on your side and the other resting on the top of your arm; if you're sitting, crossing your legs in the opposite direction of the person you're dealing with. As soon as possible, leave the room and head in the opposite direction ~ being mindful once again to not re-play what just happened over and over again in your mind. And no telling tales, either!

An underlying premise to all of this is something well worth noting. Our natural state of being is to be healthy, robust Citizens of the World. Anything else is contrary to our natural state of being. We can cultivate this with our day-to-day wish to be all that we can be, fulfilling the Divine Destiny our Soul envisioned prior to birth. Stuart Wilde, a man of great skill and humor, would say that we could be in the middle of a war zone, and if our personal vibration was higher than the vibration of the war, nothing could ever hurt us. He went on to say that we could be walking down the street, with bombs going off on the other side of the street, and we would remain perfectly healthy and well ~ untouched by the mayhem…actually not even noticed by the warring forces! It takes internal focus, minding our own business, and remaining in a state of ongoing wellness and hopefulness. But that is our task at hand, and I am willing to practice that every day as if my Life depends on it because it most certainly does.

\*\*\*\*\*\*\*\*\*\*\*\*\*\*\*\*\*\*\*\*\*\*\*\*\*\*\*\*

**Mind your own business.** You are not in this Life for anyone else. You are here to understand yourself and your connection to the Divine. The issue of judgment is always a tremendous problem. As you learn to focus on yourself and your Life journey, you will automatically have less time to focus on judging someone else. This also eliminates useless "mind chatter." Once you can establish better boundaries, you'll have so much more love, light, and power for yourself and to share with others.

EXERCISE: Learn to work with Mantras and or Affirmations to occupy your mind rather than allowing yourself to float into other people's thoughts or lives. Try these: "My Life counts. My Life matters. I come first in my Life. The focus is on myself. My Life is a special journey. My Life has meaning and value. I am allowed to be happy, whole, healthy and abundant in every way!"

\*\*\*\*\*\*\*\*\*\*\*\*\*\*\*\*\*\*\*\*\*\*\*\*\*\*\*\*

**In the TOLTEC Tradition** you are taught to "root" yourself into the ground, making yourself unmovable and unshakable. After you have done that, you can then open fully through the heart and align yourself with your pure essence self.

EXERCISE: Stand up and feel all of the parts of your feet touching the floor, rooted to the floor. After that has been established, begin to direct the breath through the entire body, anchoring your energy through the Crown Chakra at the top of the head, right down through the feet and into the center of Mother Earth. Once you feel yourself to be totally anchored, then deliberately open your Heart Chakra at the center of your chest and ask to be aligned with your pure Essence Self. You are now ready and prepared to move out into the World, tackling any situation within a self-induced state of perfectly anchored Life Force Energy.

**When the time has come to disconnect from someone,** here is the perfect technique to work with.

EXERCISE: Called the Karmic Releasing Exercise, you would proceed in the following manner. Visualize the person you're working with and call out their name three times to get the attention of their Higher Self. Then say their name with each of the following statements:

_____ I thank you for all past Life experiences.

_____ I forgive you for all karma, past and present.

_____ I release you from playing any Karmic role for me.

God Bless YOU!! God Bless ME!!

After completing this exercise, do not dwell on it, do not journal about it. And by all means, do not tell your friends and family, or you'll only stir up the person all over again.

\*\*\*\*\*\*\*\*\*\*\*\*\*\*\*\*\*\*\*\*\*\*\*\*\*\*\*\*\*

**When there is a bothersome issue that needs attention**, the following statements are very helpful.

EXERCISE: "I cast the burden of this situation with _____ on the God within, and I go free!"

"As I release myself to the Light, I release you (insert name) to the Light. You have no power over me!"

And here in our Western culture, the strongest statement of protection you can ever make is: "In the name of Jesus Christ, God Bless You! You have no power over me!"

Followed by whatever is appropriate: Get away from me! You are not allowed to be near me!"

**Sometimes people just don't get the message to leave.** In a case such as this, where you've tried to end a relationship or send someone packing and they simply can't or won't respect your wishes, the following technique will work.

EXERCISE: Only do this in the shower and never while sitting in the tub. After you're all wet, hair included, call in an image of the person in question. See them suspended in midair in front of you in the shower, and then proceed with your dominant hand to wrap them in wide, darkly colored ace bandages. Wrap them from head to toe and then from side to side just like a mummy. When they are completely wrapped up tight, push outward and upward with your dominant hand as you make the statement:

"You have no power over me, and I demand that you leave my Life now!"

Continue pushing them away forcefully until you actually feel the individual in question leaving your energy field. You may even imagine having an image of them floating out of the shower completely. It is usually necessary to repeat this exercise several times until a complete disconnection has been made. This is especially true if the person in question has been a past sexual partner, as those ties and connections run very deep in our many layered systems.

*** While doing this work to release a person, do not talk about them to others, do not write about them in your journal, do not mention them on Social Media, and resist the urge to dwell on them in any way, or you'll be calling them right back to you.

*****************************

**Redirecting The Energy is essential**. The hardest thing to control at times is your own emotional investment in any given situation. You must suspend your emotions if you're going to be successful at psychic self- defense.

EXERCISE: Connect deeply with the fear/sadness/rage/panic in your stomach or Solar Plexus or the Heart Chakra, and then redirect that energy up to the Third Eye. This is done with the breath. Stand up tall, connect with the feelings, breathe into them, and then shoot them up to the forehead, right to the Third Eye. Then allow your decisions and actions to come from the neutral space of the intellect rather than the emotions. It takes practice and a willingness to change, but this does work.

*****************************

In all of these situations, the goal is always self-care while at the same time wishing no deliberate harm to anyone else. It's important in Life to maintain a balanced state of awareness while also exhibiting kindness to ourselves and others.

I have discovered for myself that when I approach a situation or another person with the highest hopes and a sense of internal peace, the highest and best outcome is achieved.

What we project from within our own internal bundle of electromagnetic energy out into the World is the only possible thing we can ever hope to draw back to us. Project hate ~ receive hate back. Project fear ~ receive fear back. If I am deliberately holding myself accountable to a higher standard, and I am aware of who I am as a Child of God, walking and working in the Light of the Divine, then I am apt to show up with integrity and calmness. In any encounter, I always do my best to project an essence of welcoming kindness. I will deliberately continue projecting that until I am confronted with something to the contrary. When that occurs, I am going to move forward with all of my Psychic Self Defense techniques until I once again feel peaceful, safe, and calm.

Project love and hope ~ receive back love and hope.

Project equanimity and peace ~ receive back equanimity and peace.

## Action Steps

Using the journal pages provided here or working in your own journal, ask yourself if reading this chapter has inspired you to take better care of yourself on etheric levels?

Which exercises speak to me louder than the others? Why?

Which exercise in particular can I envision myself using immediately?

Are there any candidates in my Life who I feel warrant the Karmic Releasing Exercise?

How has reading this chapter strengthened my resolve to take better care of myself?

# Chapter Eleven

## Wrapping It All Up

Thanks for hanging in there and making it all the way to Chapter Eleven ~ I appreciate that so much since I wasn't sure I'd make it this far, either!

## You Are A Divine Being

The Number ONE take away from this book is that you are a Divine Being created in the image of The Divine. Call that Divine Essence, anything that works for you: G-D, GOD, Eliohim, Jehovah, Heavenly Father, Allah, or the Brahman, El Shaddai, Jesus the Christ, or choose from the countless other sacred names scattered throughout recorded history. If you are afraid of believing in God because you've been hurt, abandoned, or disappointed by your Life so far, then make up a name that works for you and use it daily! As Professor Dumbledore told Harry Potter, "Those who ask for help at Hogwarts, always receive it." The point is that we all need a guiding force to help hold us accountable and to help us remain motivated as we are on the way to manifesting our best hopes, wishes, and dreams. I am quite confident that **the God of my understanding** will hear **you** and **me**, too, whenever we call out, no matter what name we use. I just know it.

As my friend Jimmy reminded me the other day, his beloved grandmother used to say, "It never matters what the name above the door says. What matters is that God is in the hearts of the people inside." Thank you to Jimmy's grandmother for that mouth full of wisdom. I was the child who was asked to leave my Catholic school classroom because I innocently asked the Sister, "Where do all the children from China go when they die if they weren't baptized in the Catholic Church. Can't they go to Heaven too? They didn't know about us yet, so it's not their fault."

It took me years to realize that the terrified, stricken look on Sister's face had more to do with her own lack of preparedness than it did about my seven-year-old, innocent question. Bless her.

In the Dalai Lama' s "Mind and Life" conversations, he reminds us that there is too much anxiety, fear, and worry on the Planet today, and not nearly enough sense of our Oneness. It's easy to get lost in the crowd of seven (7) billion plus human beings especially if we are struggling to maintain a singular focus on just us. However, when we move into the concept of an entire Planet of sentient beings, and that we are all ONE at our core, Life can suddenly become more doable. Oneness Conscience means we are all ONE MIND/ONE HEART/ONE LIFE in the eyes of the Divine. It is up to us to call on that sense of unity, one empowering thought at a time. But we must take some positive action forward. It's up to us.

Quantum Physics has proven to us now that we are all indeed ONE, and when one part of a field of energy changes, it automatically affects the entire field. In other words, I may not be able to heal the entire World, but I most certainly can work at healing the entire World within myself. And that in turn has the potential to spread outward in an ever-widening circle of goodness and health, not just for myself, but for you, too.

I was not raised in a hopeful household. On the contrary, my upbringing was full of fear and ominous clouds of doubt, shame, and alcoholism. But by the Grace of God, something deep inside of me knew otherwise. And through one brilliant and unusual circumstance after another, I was led to better and better circumstances. Did it happen overnight? Of course not ~ but it did happen, and consequently, I am the product of so much grace and kindness and love that I was able to **simply continue**. If you are currently in dire circumstances, please believe me when I say that we get big points for just staying upright and putting one foot in front of the other. Momentum builds upon itself, and so does grace and healing.

# That Internal Spark of Knowingness

I was born with that spark of knowingness that kept urging me onward. Even at the bleakest moment, I knew God and the Angels were watching and waiting, urging me onward to succeed. Gratitude has always lived in my heart, and I have always been sincere in my immediate thanks to anyone and everyone who ever helped me. As I grew and began in earnest to look for my own "good face," I have always given back whenever I could to love and encourage others to find their right path.

*If the only prayer you ever say in your entire Life is thank you, it will be enough.* ~ Meister Eckhart

**Stop whining and become your own advocate.**

Shake it up and look outside your usual boxes. Go somewhere different and find some new people to share with and to learn from. Listen to some new voices, go to a new gym, a new church on the other side of town, take a walk in a new park or go to the zoo and talk to every animal you see. Become a community leader, walk around your neighborhood, and say "hello" to anyone you pass. We can get stale so quickly if we only live in the same rut, which is never a healthy approach. It's a safe approach if you never want to be anything else, better or bigger or kinder or more knowledgeable than you are now. (Now that's a bummer!) Act like you matter and act as if the world is your oyster. Ask sincerely that your "God of the present moment" immediately inspires you and leads you in the perfect right direction for NOW.

*Believe you can do "it" ~ then give it all you've got!*

When my mother died, and I was just a child, I had no clue the Universe would send me a "second mother" by way of my boyfriend's Mom ~ Lucy Marie Edey. Was I still mad, scared, and heartbroken about my own loss? ABSOLUTELY! And I told God all about it many times. I acted out and got stupid, and I got drunk and acted like a fool. And then Mrs. Edey loved me like a daughter and she began to teach me all the things about being a woman that my own mother hadn't had the time nor the wherewith all to teach. I know both of these amazing women who loved me dearly, and so well, are on their own Heavenly perches ~ I feel them sometimes together and sometimes apart ~ but still loving me from afar, knowing they made their mark on me and I carry them both with me forever. As saddened and unhappy as my own mother was, Mom was a bundle of energy and oh so hopeful ~ and full of childlike mischief. She immediately called me "Rosie" and even though I had been raised to never ever allow for a nickname, I suddenly loved being called Rosie by this special beam of Godly Light.

Mom was a God Send for sure, but I have had countless others along the way, and I'm betting you have, too. Who are they, or were they? Jog your memory and start making a list right now.

My Magical Mentors:

#1

#2

#3

#4

#5

# Everything Matters ~ Every Little Thing

This is no small statement: numbers matter, colors matter, the phase of the Moon matters and so does your willingness to stretch your mind/brain system to let new things in.

For instance, why do you think I chose (5) five Magical Mentors? Go back and look at the information on Numerology, and you'll discover that the # 5 is a physical number referred to as "The Adventurer" and governed by the Planet Mars. It's full of curiosity, physical stamina, and it represents the letters E ~ N & W. See how it all ties together? The more we know and the more we understand, the broader our Life concepts become.

Imagine, if you will, a magical spiral of energy that is in constant motion, and it's trying to get your attention. Hidden within this magical spiral of energy are all of the keys to the kingdom. Your kingdom. But it calls for your cooperation, your awareness, and your disciplined attention, and your ability to S – T – R –E – T –C – H way beyond the constructs of your own family of origin belief systems.

I think it's pitiful that countless generations have used Religion as a fearful shield to "protect us from Sin!" The real sin to me is that this shameful ploy continues, giving greater strength and belief to the awful things **that might happen** in Life rather than encouraging the good that comes from self-exploration. One of the best things I've ever heard is that the definition of a GURU is simply, "A being with an endless repertoire of responses." No cookie-cutter fearful statements of shame, guilt or going to that ubiquitous place called HELL. "Watch out, you'll go to hell if you don't go to church!" "Well, you're doomed if you get divorced. You'll be locked out of Heaven for sure!" And the saddest of all, "You know if you masturbate, you're going straight to HELL." ~ Said no one ever who had the chance to explore their own fabulous body and its many responses to appropriate stimulation.

I do know that parents and older family members do not intentionally set out to harm children, but it's simply a reflection of their own fears and what they heard growing up. This is your chance to change all of that as you intentionally *FLIP* your own internal dialogue. Please don't waste a moment ~ your real Life is waiting for you.

Take a moment to reflect on the things you'd like to give up from your own Family of Origin.

## Releasing Old Family Patterns

#1.

#2.

#3.

#4.

#5.

Good job! Now when something pops up, and it will, be ready to answer it back immediately. One day, years ago, as I was looking in the bathroom mirror, I distinctly heard my mother's voice saying, "Women who wear glasses should never wear earrings!" Even as that old pang of shame and guilt hit my Solar Plexus, I had enough therapy and training under my belt to respond immediately with, "Oh hush,

Mom, that's so silly! I do wear glasses and I wear earrings every day. And I like it." That's the last time I ever heard that or any comment like it from my beloved mother.

Our eyes glance at a million things in the course of a day and our ears are listening to every sound. What of those many things are you meant to pay attention to? Our internal radar "hears" and picks up on countless messages in the course of a day. Which ones are meant for you to pay attention to? My immediate answer to that would be to ask your own Deep Internal Body Wisdom, "Is that for me? Is it even relevant, and if so, what do I do next?" If you hear a response, and it feels true, act on it as soon as possible, allowing for the next step to reveal itself.

As you continue to eliminate distractions to your authentic growth ~ such as old Family Of Origin patterns, and consciously working at releasing those traumas and patterns that hold you back, your level of internal communication will get clearer. Think of it like developing a new skill. As with any new endeavor, practice, repetition, and trial and error are all your friends. The more you learn to listen, the better you'll get at creating your own internal dialogue.

## Creating Your Healing Team

A huge part of finding your true self is creating the right team of people who understand your body, your mind, and most of all, your Spirit. Don't settle for anyone but the best Primary Care Physician. To me, that is someone who understands all of your needs and not just medical issues.

Ideally, you'll find someone like my Primary Care Physician who is as intuitive as she is gifted medically. She did not flinch at my battery of questions I use when first getting acquainted with any new provider.

#1. What is your birth date, the day, place and time if known?

As I explain this is my area of expertise, and it helps me know how to communicate with you and who you are to me. If the potential provider is not forthcoming with this or scoffs at the notion that I might require this, we have a brief relationship.

#2. Why did you choose this specialty, and who was the major motivator/mentor in your early education? This usually provides an opportunity for true communication between patient and doctor and allows us both a deeper glimpse into what makes us both who we are.

#3. What are your hobbies? If the proposed provider tells you they have no hobbies, and that they are only devoted to their work ~ RUN FOR THE DOOR. They are just not right mentally. If you're licensed to cut into another human being's body, you'd better have a hobby that captivates your creative energy and gives you something to look forward to.

I've been privileged to be surrounded by some amazing Physicians, all of whom have helped me to hone those first questions for any new provider.

My healing team also includes a Chiropractor, a Homeopathic Healer, a Chinese Medical Physician, and a Massage Therapist.

## My Chiropractor

I worked with my Chiropractor for nineteen years, and over that time, we developed a close working relationship. The late Dr. Luby Chambul of the Chambul Wellness Center in Nashville was curious, compassionate, and patient-oriented. Not only was he a Chiropractor, but he was also a fully trained and licensed Acupuncture Physician, working with Applied Kinesiology, Genetic testing and Methylation therapy, as well as Neuro Feedback, Neural Emotional Technique and Electro-Acupuncture. With such a broad base to his practice, Dr. Chambul attended to all of the functions of my physical, mental, and my emotional body.

## My Homeopathic Physician

I've been privileged to work with an elegantly trained Homeopathic Physician named Anke Nowicki from Light Partners, LLC since 1993. Her work is all inclusive and considers every aspect of my personal Life. Using the basis of her diagnosis for me, I have been able to seek the appropriate care and treatment from not only non-traditional but allopathic caregivers. Because of her extensive skill set including Light and Color Therapy, Bio-Energetic Research, and Heart Intelligence Theory, her all-encompassing approach has unraveled many mysteries for me to work with.

## My Chinese Physician

My Chinese Physician, Dr. Wrai Luk of Houston, Texas, was trained in his native Hong Kong and is a superb "reader of the human energy field." He is no longer accepting new patients, but I encourage you to seek out a classically trained Chinese Physician who treats with both acupuncture and individually prepared herbal teas prepared especially to treat your current condition. Dr. Luk was referred to me by Anke Nowicki in 2007 when I was experiencing mysterious symptoms no medical doctor could properly diagnose. I've been working with him ever since.

## My Clinical Nutritional Consultant

Having a well-trained and eagle-eyed Nutritional Consultant such as Douglas Fleckman on my side has been an ongoing journey toward wholeness. Referred to me by Anke Nowicki in 2008, Douglas has come to know me literally, inside and out! Relentless in his search for why the body is responding in any given manner, he is a master at creating exactly the right nutritional program for every client. And he's a good sparring partner too, especially when I've occasionally disagreed with his approach.

## My Massage Therapist

I am abundantly Blessed to work with another classically trained natural healer, Pauline Diaz. Trained in Classis Swedish Massage as well as Cranial Sacral work, Pauline is an expert at "reading the body" and remaining in a constant "conversation" with my body during every treatment. I have long ago learned not to argue with her process or her determination of what my body needs during any given treatment.

There you have it, a bird's eye view of my personal Healing Team. And yes, it is all self-pay as none of this is covered by traditional medical insurance. Many years ago when I was moving my practice from West Palm Beach, Florida, to Virginia and ultimately to Nashville, I had an argument with my insurance agent and lost insurance coverage. What started out as a nightmare resulted in my personal search for the right healthcare for my particular needs. I don't advise this course of action for you, but I'm simply pointing it out as yet one more example of how Divine Order is always working on our behalf.

I have been "told" ~ read that as Spiritually directed ~ to end this book with a significant gift from my teacher, Shri Bodhisattva called the Sacred Flame Initiation. We used this at ARC at the opening of many sacred occasions, and it always left me feeling deeply loved and at one with all that is. Perhaps you might consider using this for yourself or introducing it to your Spiritual community. You will need a white candle, and matches, and hopefully be in a setting that allows for concentration and focus.

# The Sacred Flame Initiation

Begin by centering yourself with deep breathing. When you are ready and focused, begin with a series of three "OMS" as you prepare to light the flame. Then light the candle as you say:

The Sacred Flame is visible,

May all hearts be open and reminded ~

Light is my very nature, I AM only Light!

When the Universe manifests itself,

Verily then, it is I that shines.

I AM the Light of the World!

As you prepare to finish, conclude the ceremony with another series of three "OMS."

Well, there you have it, the final chapter. For me, the problem with writing one final chapter is my desire to "add just one more thing"! But alas, there are deadlines, and it's time to wrap this up today. Thank you for allowing this dream of my heart to land in your hands and on your screen. My wish for you is abundant health in mind, body, and spirit and that you enjoy every moment of this Holy Privilege called Life.

Blessings to you and to all those you hold dear, Rosemary

# Final Offering

## The Emergency Toolkit

ROSEMARY'S EMERGENCY "TOOL KIT" for Sanity, Health and Safety

I've been privileged to look at Life through a lens many never have the chance to see through. In my World, we are surrounded by thousands of Angelic Beings whose only task is to keep us alive ~ safe ~ well and as protected as we allow them to keep us. There are multiple layers to Life, and only the densest are visible to the naked eye. Expanding our vision and our consciousness to include multiple dimensions of Life is a journey of growth and expansion. Like so many of us, I was born into a family that observed a Religious tradition based in shame, fear and guilt. As an Irish Catholic, the concept of "Original Sin" was simply a known concept that was accepted as an underlying truth to every Catholic's Life. It was only as I got older and was exposed to other belief systems that I began to form my own concepts of Life as a deserving Child of God who was not born into anything but Love, Light and Hope. It has become so apparent to me now, more than ever before, that we all need a better, more finely tuned internal sense of our own worth/value, safety and protection than at any previous time on our beloved School House Planet Earth.

I have a deep and abiding belief in God, but I've always understood that God relies on the assistance, wisdom and presence of countless Ascended Masters. These Light Beings, including The Great White Brotherhood, (never to be confused with any racist humans) are beings of grace and power who spread Spiritual teachings and are focused only on our highest good and our personal Spiritual evolution. These beings are also known as Masters of Ancient Wisdom, Ascended Masters, the Church Invisible and are often referred to as **The Illumined Ones**. These beings, along with all of the Arch Angels, can be called upon at a moment's notice to come to our aid. If we don't ask, these Light Beings simply stand by and witness our sometimes inspired, but oftentimes, foolish actions. It is a wise thing to know when we need help and that it is there for the asking. Humility and an awareness that **we don't know what we don't know** can be among our most powerful assets, but only if we have the courage to move forward and **ASK** for help.

Take what you want from my Emergency Tool Kit, you may need to read it a couple of times. You've picked this up for a reason, so why not trust the process and at least give it a try? It's called Divine Order In Action for a good reason.

#1. BREATHE ~ Breathe as if your Life depends on it because it most certainly does. From that first Breath of Life as we pop out of the womb, to that last breath as we finish this Life's journey, our breath gives us the chance to live our best lives in ease and harmony. If you think about it, we oftentimes hold our breath with a gasp when we've been startled, or our concentration has been suddenly broken. The very moment you realize you've been holding your breath, breathe from your nose right down to your toes and exhale fully through your mouth with a deep sigh of relief. If the concept of breath work feels particularly meaningful to you, refer to Chapter Four: Breath Work for more detailed information and instructions.

#2. Imagine believing this: Divine Order Prevails and the Best is Yet to Come. Thoughts are things and the energy trail they create make up 98% of the story of our lives, so you've got nothing to lose by changing or at least creating an up-grade in your own thinking. Check out the teachings of "Abraham~Hicks" on YouTube, and if it resonates with you, listen daily. A profound example of this was brought home to me many years ago as a friend's father had been diagnosed with Stage IV colon cancer at Roswell Park Memorial Institute, a pre-eminent cancer treatment and research center in Buffalo, New York. They give a battery of tests to each in-coming cancer patient to determine their likely recovery rate. Their margin of error is quite slim, at less than 1.5%. Their results are just as accurate today as they were in the 1970s. The takeaway being that it's all up to the attitude and belief patterns of each and every patient, whether they'll survive, thrive, or not fare well at all. And to know that one's mindset has so much power over the end result to me is a strong enough motivation to be more deliberate with my thoughts and my emotions around any issue. If and when I am dealing with an illness of any kind, there are only four or five people I trust with the details because I know they will be an aid to my recovery as opposed to "seeing me through the lens of the temporary illness currently moving through me." Please consider that for yourself in times of need, perhaps limiting how many people you pull into your circle of trust. My friend's dear father believed that his diagnosis was a death sentence, and in his case, it proved to be true.

#3. If you are ever in need of immediate physical protection, this statement: **"In the Name of Jesus Christ, God Bless you!"** is a most powerful command, especially here in the United States or in any predominantly Christian country. When it is accompanied by making the Sign of the Cross on the back of the neck ~ either your own neck or an offending party, the protection is strengthened ten-fold. The effect is immediate and **no harm** can come to you from any outside source. If physical touch is not possible, use your powerfully vivid imagination to "draw" the Sign of the Cross. Equally effective, though not as dramatic, is simply raising your hand in the **"Stop Sign"** position as you say out loud, "NO, that is not happening ~ go away now, you are not allowed here ~ you have no power over me!"

#4. Believing you are a Divine Being, a literal Child of the Divine, and that you are loved by God, no matter what, is very protective. Please claim that status, even if you're not one-hundred percent sure of it yourself **just yet**. When you combine that belief with your favorite prayer from childhood, no matter what the tradition you come from, it increases the protection as it enhances your sense of well-being. My go- to prayer is the "Hail Mary, full of grace, The Lord is with thee! Blessed art thou amongst women and Blessed is the Fruit of Thy Womb, Jesus. Holy Mary, Mother of God, pray for our sinners now, and at the hour of our death. Amen" I usually follow it with the Glory Be, "Glory Be to the Father, the Son and the Holy Spirit, Amen"

Choose a prayer that speaks to your heart without reservation, and one that flawlessly flows through your being without hesitation.

#5. Call on Lord Michael the Archangel to protect your home, business, vehicle and most importantly, your personal self. I've attached the full Blessing for you. Please practice with it, memorize it, and use it liberally on a daily basis so you are always protected. The youngest person I've ever taught this to was five years old at the time, and he still uses it now at the age of seventeen. The oldest was a gentleman named DeWayne who was 86, his wife said it was the last thing she heard him say as he was passing into the Heavens with a peaceful smile on his face.

I have no doubt he was in the presence of many Angels, including Lord Michael the Arch Angel.

> *Lord Michael to the front,*
> *Lord Michael to the rear,*
> *Lord Michael to the right,*
> *Lord Michael to the left,*
> *Lord Michael above,*
> *Lord Michael below,*
> *Lord Michael, Lord Michael wherever I go!*

#6. Call on all four of these Arch Angels to create a protective unit that will surround you for balance and protection. Ask Lord Michael to stand in front of you with his back to you; call upon Arch Angel Raphael to stand at your right with his back to you; call upon Arch Angel Uriel to stand behind you with his back to you and Arch Angel Gabriel to stand to your left with his back to you as well. I use this daily whenever I have to go to a busy place and I want extra protection. Many years ago I was told these are the primary Angels of Judaism and then I could not find any record of that being a true thing ~ until today. The reference comes from a piece called the "Gracia Nasi" and a portion of it is given here for your reference.

## Gracia Nasi

> *In the Name of Hashem, God of Israel:*
> *May Michael be at my right, Gabriel at my left,*
> *Uriel before me, and Raphael behind me;*
> *And above my head, the Presence of God.*

This is a bedtime prayer invoking the protection of the Archangels: Michael performing His unique miracles; Gabriel, the emissary of His almighty power; Uriel, who bears the Light of God before you; Raphael, who brings you healing from Him. Above your head is the Presence of God himself.

I was beyond excited when I found this, buried in my files as so many things are ~ and I laughed at myself for creating my own take on this, using "my guy" Lord Michael in the front and Raphael to my right, just a nod to my dear dyslexic, ADHD self. What a hoot we all are!!

#7. The realm of Personal Guardian Angels is yet another level of this astounding Angelic protection. I've had the privilege of working with a gifted intuitive who discovered the name of my Guardian Angel; however, she is no longer practicing. You can perhaps discover this for yourself through your own meditative experience or seek out a practitioner gifted in this area. Or you can simply call out to your "Guardian Angel", trusting they will be there, just as they have always been throughout the ages.

#8. Use of the "I Am" Incantations immediately opens us up to union with the essence of Saint Germain. "I **Rosemary**, do hereby withdraw all power which I have given to other people or to situations to control my experience in all areas of my Life. I am a victim no longer! I am in control of my experiences, and by knowing this, and choosing this, I start myself on the road to perfect peace and joyous fulfillment in all areas of my Life." The entire list of Incantations is included in Chapter Five for your personal work. These are not only empowering, but they are ageless in scope.

#9. The use of Affirmations has long been considered to be a powerful moment-by-moment method of training the mind to deliberately attract the best possible state of consciousness. Believing in the theory of "like attracts like", and that we live in a World where the "Law of Attraction" is in motion constantly, creating and maintaining the best mind set possible is a must. A detailed list of my favorite Affirmations and positive statements can be found in Chapter Five: Affirmations, Incantations and Mantras to help put your thoughts on the right track for success and inner peace. Begin jotting down your own favorites in **your journal** to have them handy at a moment's notice.

#10. MAP work with The Co-Creative Brotherhood can be Life- changing and not only healing to human beings but to the Planet we call "Home." MAP is short for "**M**edical **A**ssistance **P**rogram", an entire system of interactivity between humanity and Nature. If you're not familiar with this remarkable system, find this resource online. This is a miraculous program that I have worked with since 1992, created by Machelle Small Wright from the Perelandra Center for Nature Research in Virginia. If this resonates with you, it will open you to realms of extraordinarily powerful manifestations of Life. The book is entitled, *MAP: Medical Assistance*

*Program*, and it is available through Perelandra or on Amazon. Again, the author is Machelle Small Wright.

#11. EFT – Emotional Freedom Technique. Use any method you're familiar with to tap out fear, isolation or worries. First brought into common usage in 1997 and created by Gary Craig, EFT is efficient, easy to master and a technique you will always have at your disposal. Working with the natural meridian ~ or energy lines of the body ~ one well-placed tap can set into motion an all-body response, resulting in an immediate sense of tranquility and a release from anxiety, tension and fear. It has been a privilege to use this effectively for many years with people of every age and background. *The Tapping Solution* with Nick Ortner is also an excellent resource.

#12. In the last twenty years, REIKI HEALING has become quite commonly accepted not only in alternative healing settings, but also in traditional hospital settings as well. It has become quite popular with many of the nurses I've met with over the years. The Traditional **Usui Shiki Ryoho** System of Natural Healing is taught in 3 levels: First Degree for physical, hands-on healing, Second Degree for absent healing at a distance and the Third or final Mastership level. If you have attained the Second-Degree level you can easily use the First and Second characters to "pave the way ahead for yourself." By literally projecting these first 2 symbols, along with their meanings, you will be commanding the forces of the Universe to keep yourself safe, focused and steady. The first principle of Reiki is "Healer, Heal Thyself." Another brilliant system of healing comes from the Kahuna Priests of Hawaii and is called **HUNA**, offering techniques for Karmic cleansing and problem solving. Both of these brilliant systems can be accessed by a Google search for resources in your area.

#13. The use of a Personal Mantram, or Mantra, can be the literal "icing on the cake" in terms of an "Emergency Tool Kit 101." Throughout the ages, every major religion has used a Mantram, and most often, more than one. Raised as an Irish Catholic, the *"Hail Mary"*, used in reference to the Blessed Mother, has always been one of my favorites. In fact, when I am in any kind of jeopardy, it's the first thing that comes to mind for me. It's so automatic that I often simply find myself repeating it over and over until any sense of unrest has passed. The *"Ava Maria"* is also a traditional Catholic Mantra, and if it feels good to you ~ claim it. In India, one of the oldest and best known Mantrams is **"Rama"** and translates to one of the names of the Lord that comes from a word meaning "joy" or even to "rejoice." Hence, the use of *"Rama, Rama, Rama"* is calling on the source of joy within our own hearts. It is said that **"Rama"** is the very Mantram that was used by Mahatma Gandhi, the famous Indian lawyer turned political ethicist who employed nonviolent resistance to lead the successful campaign for India's independence from Great Britain. It is also worth noting here that when we connect with a specific tradition, we have the ability to also connect with the Spiritual vibration of **that Soul** no matter where they are on the continuum of Life, thus enhancing our own power and adding a deeper layer of meaning to our own practice.

I've felt a kinship to Judaism my whole Life and used to attend Synagogue with a special friend in my childhood. My favorite Jewish Mantram means "Blessed art thou, O Lord" in English and is **"Barukh Attah Adonai."** As with any Mantra, the sense of connection and empowerment increases with repetition. Carry your Mantra with you 24 hours a day, making a deeper connection with each and every repetition, allowing its warmth and depth to penetrate all of your senses. The familiar Buddhist Mantram, **"Om mani padme hum,"** is also a superb choice, especially for those seeking a deeper heart connection to the Self. *Mani* means "jewel" and *padme* means "lotus"; together the words refer to "the jewel in the lotus of the heart."

When embarking on the use of a Personal Mantram, take your time and feel the internal vibration when you say it out loud or silently. Use any of the Mantras I've listed here, or seek out others in Holy books, choosing one that has been sanctified by tradition. Once you have chosen, stay with it for at least six months, avoiding the urge to jump around. This is scared work and should be approached as such. And please avoid the temptation to create your own Mantra, relying instead on traditions. The use of Mantras is discussed in greater depth in Chapter Five: "Affirmations, Incantations and Mantras."

#14. Another useful discipline working with Mantras is a repetition of the "72 Names of God." Coming to us from the ancient Kabbalistic Jewish traditions, the 72 Names are each 3-letter sequences that act like an index to specific, Spiritual frequencies. Done reverently and with a sense of devotion to the inner doorways/realms, which open to each name, this can be a useful and deeply meaningful meditation. Even though this is of Jewish origin, when one is a devoted Spiritual student, one realizes that the Divine speaks to us through many voices. Don't worry about not being able to pronounce the names correctly, just touch each name with a fingertip ~ moving right to left. If a particular name evokes a stronger sensation within you, simply rest there, absorbing the vibration into your being. The entire list can be accessed by a simple Google search. As you ponder these names, take the time to sense whether or not you have any emotional connection to this resource. You will know this rather quickly, and if not, at least you will have been touched by The Divine in a new way. These 72 Named sequences have the extraordinary power to overcome the laws of Nature in all forms, including human nature. Please remember that you do not have to know how to pronounce the names to receive the Spiritual healing and vibration. If one in particular resonates with you at a deep level, then look it up online for the pronunciation and the meaning. If you are led to dig deeper into this extraordinary work, which is the formula Moses used to overcome the laws of Nature which had been hidden in the Zohar for 2000 years, read, "The 72 Names of God: Technology for The Soul." Your Life will be enhanced immeasurably and your whole vibration elevated considerably for the better.

#15. On a lighter note, if there is someone in your Life that just gets on your last nerve, here's an easy and gentle way to contain them. Imagine the person in question standing in front of you and begin to wrap them in layer upon layer of PINK COTTON CANDY. Make a lovely imaginary game of it, smiling to yourself as you deliberately and with **sincere intention**, "wrap" up the person quite securely in this gooey, sweet, all sugary concoction. As you take apart these Elements, you're using the colors of white (which contains all colors on the spectrum) with red (which is the color of creation) to create pink (the color of love); now in combination with a sticky, sugary "glue" that will hold to the person in question any type of projected energy they might be tempted to send your way. Once you've been deliberate about your intentions, it'll only take you a few seconds to "refresh" the PINK COTTON CANDY whenever the need arises. Over time you might be surprised to realize the person's impact on you has been dramatically reduced to "nothingness." Be mindful to NOT send any mean-spirited thoughts, however, just pink sugary, sweet glue ONLY.

#16. An easy but profound technique is to simply "turn away" and to not engage with a rageful, bullying or annoying individual. You can turn your chair around, turn your body away from the person in question, or just leave the room entirely. My wonderfully wise friend Mitzie taught me a statement that rocked my world, "Oh, I just don't go into it that deep"! This came after I overheard her patiently explain to an older couple about a potential PT appointment time NOT being available to them. Three times the people in question asked for the same time, only to have Mitzie patiently explain that spot was not open. At some point, the woman then asked about an alternate time (which had been the first thing Mitzie had offered), and the deal was done. I, as a nosey by-stander, was exhausted from the ordeal of eavesdropping, while my patient and composed friend remained cool as a cucumber. Hence, her brilliant response, "Oh, I just don't go into it that deep!" Proving once again that we simply MUST laugh at ourselves, often, as we keep on learning every day.

#17. From my work with Reiki Master and Auric Healer, Jeanne Greening, I learned the value of internal emotional clearing followed by wrapping myself up with Saran Wrap. Jeanne literally wrapped me up in actual Saran Wrap on many occasions since I am such a vibrant psychic sponge. I have taken this concept and created a visualization where I pull out a gigantic piece of Saran Wrap, encrusted with small tumbled Black Tourmalines for protection and safety. I imagine wrapping myself from the top of my head ~ leaving small openings for the eyes, ears, nose and mouth ~ then going down the full length of my body, crisscrossing like a mummy. You can make as many revolutions around the body as you feel are necessary. If you're about to do something that has you more unsettled than usual, employ the tools listed here from #3 to #7 to make you feel as safe and protected as possible. Then relax and believe you're FINE and SAFE.

#18. My esteemed Acupuncture Physician, Dr. Wrai Luk from Houston, Texas, taught me a while back that simply clapping our hands together with vigor clears out a lot of debris. The theory is that clapping mimics a whole-body acupuncture treatment, and when done 100 times per day ~ or in twenty-five times increments, it can re-set one's entire system. I use this often, especially after a tough client session, or when I simply need a refresh for myself. If you're having trouble settling down or clearing your mind/thoughts, then combine the clapping technique with washing your hands under running Water as you imagine your annoyances flushing down the drain. In this instance, using cold Water works best for me, but feel free to experiment for yourself since maybe warm Water might be better for you.

#19. This may sound too simplistic, but simply claiming that you are living your Life under Divine Law and not just as a member of the masses can be a profound Blessing. If I know I am operating under Divine Law as I go about my day, I am automatically elevated in consciousness. Thus, I am less likely to be reckless with my thoughts, emotions, my speech or in my physical actions. I Am A Child of God, and that is a very good thing!

These are presented with the intention of helping you toward a more relaxed, aware and consciously connected state of personal reality. If any of it seems too outlandish or just plain crazy ~ IGNORE THAT PART ~ and pay attention to only what feels right to you now. Perhaps at some later point, the rest of it might feel okay to you as well. Do not stress, this is meant to be helpful, and not a burden or an annoyance in any way.

I believe that we are meant to succeed, and that we are meant to be joyful, expressive beings who know we're created in the image of The Divine. Not merely just good enough, but brilliant, sparkling "Beings of Light", here on this Earth Plane to do the work of God with every breath we take and each word we speak. And we are meant to do that in a spirit of grand adventure and Divine Play. As we increase our understanding of who and what we are, what the essence of Nature and Reality are, and what our special place is within this Divine Universe, our sense of self grows in direct proportion to what we may then come to know as **our responsibility** to the Universal collective. And when all of that falls into place, Universes come together, the Heavens open and God smiles. And so it is!

# I am Enough ~ and so are You!

# Book List For Looking For My Good Face

Every book on this list has the power to change your Life for the better. The ones I've * are my special favorites.

## Astrology and Numerology References:

*Hickey, Isabel M. – *Astrology, A Cosmic Science ~ The Classic Work on Spiritual Astrology* - The perfect blending of Spirituality, Universal Laws and the transformational benefits of studying Astrology.

*Derek and Julia Parker – *The Compleat Astrologer* – A practical encyclopedic guide to Astrological Science from Ancient Mesopotamia to the modern World. Includes chart examples of well-known people.

*Jan Spiller and Karen McCoy – *Spiritual Astrology – Your Personal Path to Self-Fulfillment* – Linking the influence of the Planets to the growth of the Soul as influenced by the Solar and Lunar Eclipses.

*Charles and Suzi Harvey – *Sun Sign, Moon Sign – Discover the Key to Your Unique Personality Through the 144 Sun-Moon Combinations* – With greatest strengths, weaknesses and images for integration.

*Jodie Forrest – *The Ascendant* – A comprehensive look at your "doorway" into your chart and what you've come to learn and to teach.

*Martin Schulman – *The Ascendant – Your Karmic Doorway* – The influence, purpose and function of the Ascendant as it relates to past lives.

*Patricia G. Crossley – *Let's Learn Astrology – The First Astrology Workbook for Beginners* – A comprehensive and instructive textbook with a good format anyone can follow.

*Frederic Van Norstrand – *The Influence of the Moon in the Twelve Signs of the Zodiac* – A thoughtful metaphysical approach to Moon placement.

*Joanna Martine Woolfolk – *The Only Astrology Book You'll Ever Need* – A good look at the interaction of each Sign and placement, including all the body parts that are ruled by each of the 12 Zodiac Signs.

*Robert Kent "Buz" Myers – Getting On Time With Your Life – "On Time" teaches through the Solar/Lunar Eclipse cycles, how to get on time with your Life, as you dance your way around The Medicine Wheel of Life.

*Helen Paul & Bridget Mary O'Toole – Interpreting The Houses – Detailed descriptions of the 12 Houses of the Zodiac, the Signs on each Cusp and the influence on every Planetary placement. * A great resource!

*Claire Stickel & Kathleen McCuistion – Astrology in a Nutshell – The perfect guide for serious Astrology students; it covers it all in an easy-to-follow format, with excellent guidance.

*Joseph F. Goodavage – Write Your Own Horoscope – A scientific look at the "most ancient of all the sciences, from the beginning of time to now."

*Dane Rudhyar – An Astrological Mandala: The Cycle of Transformations and its 360 Symbolic Phases – A reinterpretation of the Sabian symbols, presenting them as a contemporary American I Ching.

*Marc Edmund Jones – How To Live With The Stars – Simple Personal Astrology – The perfect integration of the Planets, the Signs and the Houses. A must read for serious Astrology students.

*Donald H. Yott – Retrograde Planets And Reincarnation – Astrology and Reincarnation Volume I – A deep dive into the lessons of the Retrograde Planets and how we can evolve in this Lifetime.

*Derek Walters – The Art And Practice of Chinese Astrology – Ming Shu – A look at the revered place the Science of Astrology has always held in The Twelve Animals of the Chinese Zodiac.

*Lori Reid - The Complete Book Of Chinese Horoscopes – An introduction to the history of Chinese Horoscopes and their system of Lunar Months and Animal Years.

*Theodora Lau – The Handbook of Chinese Horoscopes – A thorough and thoughtful investigation into the history and actual practice of Chinese Astrology from childhood to education, career and relationships.

*Vera Scott Johnson & Thomas Wommack – *The Secrets of Numbers – A Numerological Guide To Your Character And Destiny* – A journey through the history of numbers from Genesis to the numerical path of your own Life.

*Dan Millman – *The Life You Were Born To Live – A Guide To Finding Your Life Purpose* – A transformative and Spiritual look at the value and the purpose of numbers in your Life. I refer to this book every day and consider it to be the best Numerology/Spiritual guide ever written.

## Emotional, Mental and Physical Healing Modalities:

*Barbara Ann Brennan – *Hands Of Light – A Guide to Healing Through the Human Energy Field* – An in depth look at the human energy field as understood through the Chakras, emphasizing the dynamic process of diseases and the creative process of health. An essential reference book.

*Barbara Ann Brennan – *Light Emerging – The Journey of Personal Healing* – This is a complete patient's guide to working with a wholistic healer and understanding the movement and importance of energy throughout the body.

*Linda Rector Page, N.D., Ph.D. – *Healthy Healing – A Guide to Self-Healing for Everyone* – A thorough reference for personal health options, blending traditional medical care with wholistic options.

*Louise Hay – *Heal Your Body – Metaphysical Causations For Physical Illness* – A resource guide reminding us that the point of power is always in the present moment and that our physical body responds immediately to our thoughts and our fears.

*Louise Hay – *You Can Heal Your Life* – An in-depth guide to understanding that the thoughts we think and the words we speak create our lives. Also offering an intimate look at how the author healed herself.

*** Any book by Louise Hay is worth reading.

*Naboru Muramoto - *Healing Ourselves* – Compiled and supplemented by Michael Abehsera - A guide for learning how to prevent, diagnose and treat diseases with food, herbs, and natural remedies.

*Evette Rose – Metaphysical Anatomy – Your Body Is Talking, Are You Listening?* A step-by-step guide to identifying psychosomatic patterns related to medical conditions and how to reverse the damage.

\*\*\* Any book by Evette Rose is worth reading.

*Pauline Wills – The Reflexology Manual – An Easy-To-Use Illustrated Guide To The Healing Zones of The Hands And Feet* - A wonderful resource for self-care, with illustrations and pictures for anyone to follow.

*Andreas Moritz – Timeless Secrets of Health & Rejuvenation – Breakthrough Medicine for the 21st Century –* A comprehensive look at how to unleash the natural healing power that lies dormant within us.

*Karol K. Truman – Feelings Buried Alive Never Die –* A comprehensive look at the meaning and value of energy vibrations and their influence on our health and well-being.

*Inna Segal – The Secret Language of Your Body – The Essential Guide To Health and Wellness –* Understanding the messages of your body, looking at the underlying mental, emotional and energetic causes of physical symptoms and medical conditions.

*Dr. Maria Kuman – Listen and Talk to your Body And Soul – A New Way of Health and Coping with Addiction and Depression –* Many insightful approaches combining Western medicine, along with ancient wisdom.

*Jacob Liberman, O.D., Ph.D. – Light Medicine Of The Future –* A testimony to how light-energy is profoundly capable of influencing the healing process on both the physical and the emotional level.

*Machelle Small Wright – MAP: The Co-Creative White Brotherhood Medical Assistance Program –* An integration of the involutionary input of Nature with man's evolutionary development. A literal roadmap to better health and emotional security, working in harmony with Mother Nature and the Angelic Realm.

\*\*\* Any book by Machelle Small Wright is worth reading.

*Bessel Van Der Kolk, M.D. – *THE BODY KEEPS THE SCORE* – *Brain, Mind, and Body In The Healing of Trauma.* Considered to be a masterpiece, this guide takes into account the painful aftermath of trauma to the body, the mind and the Life consequences that follow. It contains compelling data and real-Life stories of trauma to triumph in children and war veterans.

*John Bradshaw - *HOME COMING – Reclaiming and Healing Your Inner Child.* Including unique case histories and interactive techniques along with many skills to help us heal our inner child, breaking destructive family rules as we grow into our authentic selves.

*** Any book by John Bradshaw is worth reading.

*Dr. Joe Dispenza – *Breaking the Habit of Being Yourself – How to Lose Your Mind and Create a New One* – This book combines the fields of quantum physics, neuroscience, brain chemistry, biology, and genetics to show us what is truly possible for us.

*** Any book by Dr. Joe Dispenza is worth reading.

## Consciousness, Evolution and Personal Development:

*Dr. Richard Alpert, Ph.D. INTO Baba Ram Dass – *BE HERE NOW – REMEMBER.* A brilliant introduction to the personal journey of transformation that awaits us all, if we are curious and courageous.

*Gary Zukav – *The Dancing Wu Li Masters* – Science in combination with modern physics and quantum phenomena, questioning where humanity might be headed.

*Gary Zukav – *The Seat of the Soul* – An in-depth work on the values of the Soul, harmony, co-operation, sharing and reverence for Life.

*Gregg Braden – *Awakening To Zero Point: The Collective Initiation.* We are living in the midst of unprecedented changes unfolding within the Earth and we are all a part of those changes.

*Gregg Braden – *Walking Between the Worlds ~ The Science of Compassion.* A step-by-step guide to the ancient sciences of compassion and blessing. Including a close look at the Essene mysteries and ways to redefine hate, fear, separation and the role they play in our lives. This is needed today, more than ever before in history.

*Gregg Braden – DEEP TRUTH ~ Igniting the Memory of Our Origin, History, Destiny, and Fate.* For the first time in history, the future of our species rests upon the choices of a single generation. We are THAT generation.

*Coleman Barks and Michael Green – The Illuminated PRAYER, The Five-Times Prayer Of The Sufis* – According to tradition and testimony of Sufi mystics, The Prayer, or Salat, was first taught by the Angels. A lovely reminder that we are all, at our core, Children of the Divine.

*Esther and Jerry Hicks & The Teachings of Abraham – Ask and it is Given – Learning To Manifest Your Desires.* The most comprehensive volume of the first twenty years of the teachings from Abraham to humanity.

*Esther and Jerry Hicks & The Teachings of Abraham – The Vortex – Where The Law of Attraction Assembles All Cooperative Relationships.* A book that helps us to remember the process of creation and the pure, positive energy platform from which we all have come.

*Don Miguel Ruiz – The Four Agreements, A Practical Guide To Personal Freedom.* In the tradition of Toltec Wisdom, this is the perfect guide to living a Life of expression, integrity, clarity and impeccability.

*Dr. Wayne W. Dyer – The Shift – Taking Your Life From Ambition to Meaning.* Inspired by the movie of the same name, it illustrates how and why and when to make the move from theoretical ambition to action and meaning.

*Dr. Wayne W. Dyer – Your Ultimate Calling ~ Living An Inspired Life* – An important guide to the essential principles for finding our way back to who we are truly meant to be.

*Dr. Wayne W. Dyer – The Essential Wayne Dyer Collection* – An overview of the more than 40 books written by Dr. Dyer, many of which were on the New York Times Best Seller List.

*** Any book by Dr. Wayne W. Dyer is an investment in your Life.

*Eknath Easwaran – *Take Your Time ~ The Wisdom of Slowing Down, How to find peace and purpose in your Life.* A superb resource, offering us important wisdom about how to gain clarity, while remaining centered and balanced in our frantic and complicated World.

*Mark Nepo – *The Book of Awakening ~ Having the Life You Want by Being Present to the Life you Have.* Offering penetrating insights, this daily guide for authentic living offers depth, kindness and wisdom with ease and grace.

*** Any book by Mark Nepo will deeply enhance your Life.

*Eckhart Tolle – *The Power of NOW – A Guide to Spiritual Enlightenment –* An urgent invitation to leave our analytical mind and its false created self, the ego, behind, as we expand significantly into the higher realms of consciousness. A must guide for serious students of Life.

*Marianne Williamson – *The Healing of America/Healing The Soul of America* – A masterpiece of Spiritual wisdom about healing our many wounds as a Nation and as a united people.

*** Any book by this author is an excellent investment.

*Ernest Holmes – *The Science of Mind* – The basic textbook for the Worldwide Religious Science movement, this is a primary resource of Life-changing ideas, presented as a simple and practical Life philosophy. This has been an essential part of my Life's work and teaching since 1993.

********************************

Please read through this book list carefully and with intentional awareness of what is right for your Life now. In another year or two, your responses will be different, as you have allowed yourself to grow and expand into a larger expression of who and what you are destined to become. Know also that I could have easily added another ten to twenty books to the list, but the book list should never be longer than the book itself. Right?

Happy reading and exploration!
Blessings to you and to all those you hold dear,
Rosemary

This book would not have been possible without the belief, encouragement and strong financial backing of my friend, client and trusted ally, Charlie Ryan. His unfailing humor and support made this dream a reality. Thank you, Charlie, from the bottom of my very humble and grateful heart.

# ABOUT THE AUTHOR

For more than thirty years, Rosemary Cathcart has been conducting a healing practice based on traditional wisdom and ancient practices in combination with modern modalities. Incorporating her skills as an Intuitive Counselor, Astrologer, Numerologist, Hypnotherapist and as a Reader/Interpreter of the Pages of Shustah Divination and Meditation cards, she offers every client, and you ~ the reader ~ a vast array of skills and talents. Believing that there is *always a way* and that we can *change anything*, she remains hopeful and optimistic in the midst of even the most daunting circumstances. Standing on the shoulders of every teacher who has ever shared their wisdom with her, she will always be the perpetual student of Life, remaining in deep gratitude for all she has learned so far and for every precious moment of Life.

www.ingramcontent.com/pod-product-compliance
Lightning Source LLC
Chambersburg PA
CBHW041137120626
46547CB00020B/3020